PERSONAL EXPERIENCES OF S. O. SUSAG

By

S. O. SUSAG

Minneapolis, Minnesota

Printed by
FAITH PUBLISHING HOUSE
P. O. Box 518
Guthrie, OK 73044

PERSONAL EXPERIENCES OF S.O. SUSAG
By S. O. SUSAG

Copyright ©2020 by S. O. SUSAG
Printed On-Demand

All rights reserved. No part of this publication may be reproduced, stored in a retrieval system, or transmitted in any form or by any means—electronic, mechanical, photocopy, recording, or any other—except for brief quotations in printed reviews, without the prior permission of the copyright holder.

Softcover ISBN 978-1-64338-124-4
Hardcover ISBN 978-1-64338-125-1

Reformation Publishers, Inc.
14 S. Queen Street, Mt. Sterling, Kentucky 40353, USA
www.reformationpublishers.com
Email rpublisher@aol.com
Orders 1-800-765-2464
Information 859-520-3757
Text 606-359-2064
Fax 859-520-3357
Printed and bound in the United States of America

(S. O. Susag, his wife and children, taken about 1898)

FOREWORD

This book of a few of my experiences is written to show how the pioneer ministers worked, and how the Lord worked with them through his Holy Spirit. One outstanding fact in those days, when even though their training was limited, was their burning passion for souls shown in labors, fasting and prayer, and a heaven-born conviction and zeal for the truth. The Holy Spirit had revealed to them an unshaken faith in the Word of God; a faith that would not waver in the most trying and, to man, surprisingly unreasonable cases. My prayers are that this book will bring faith and encouragement to many a soul who is seeking God for help when all other help has failed.

I should not have waited so long before doing this writing, for because of that waiting the incidents are not written in the order which they should have been, and so many have been forgotten. Since many have indicated an interest in my experiences, may this book as it goes forth in Jesus' name bring honor and glory to God.

—The Author

Year 1948

PUBLISHER'S PREFACE

Ever since this book was first published for the author, S. O. Susag, by the Standard Printing Company, Guthrie, Okla., in the year of 1948, it has been in steady demand. These many testimonies of outstanding answers to prayer have been an inspiration of faith to many people, and they will continue to be an encouragement to every earnest and honest seeker for an increase of faith in God's precious promises. "Jesus Christ the same yesterday, and to day, and for ever." Hebrews 13:8.

In contemplation of printing this fourth edition, the undersigned publisher contacted S. O. Susag's daughter, Mrs. Art Rustand (Goldie Susag), and requested further information about her late father. In February, 1976, she relayed the following notes of interest to the reader:

"My father was born in Steinkjer, Norway, on March 28, 1862. He came from Norway to Minneapolis, Minn., and was in the store business for a while. In 1892, they moved to Paynesville, Minn., where they engaged in farming. After they moved to the farm he was converted, and in the year of 1895 he received his call from God to the ministry of the Word. He traveled as a missionary to the Scandinavian countries for many years. He also served as pastor in Grand Forks, N. D., and as an evangelist for years. In fact, at the time of his death, which was in Culbertson, Montana, when he was 90 years of age, he was traveling around holding services. His death was attributed to his age. He was up and around until three days prior to his passing. At the time of his death he made his home with his second wife in Medicine Lake, Montana. He died on July 8, 1952, and was buried beside his first wife (my mother) at the Church of God Cemetery near Wendell, Minnesota."

—Lawrence D. Pruitt

Guthrie, Okla., March 8, 1976

PERSONAL EXPERIENCES OF S. O. SUSAG

"And I will bring the blind by a way that they knew not; I will lead them in paths that they have not known; I will make darkness light before them, and crooked things straight. These things will I do unto them and not forsake them." (Isa. 42:16). This Scripture seems to fit into my life's experiences.

I was born in Norway. My parents were Lutherans. When I was two years of age an incident occurred which I have never forgotten. It was this: My Grandmother on my mother's side—a very godly woman—used to visit us at least once a month.

On the occasion to which I refer, as she was about to leave us, Grandmother said to my mother, "Ellen, I would like to speak to you 'under four eyes' (that is to say, privately). Does the child understand anything that is said?" Her reply was, "No, he doesn't understand." Then Grandmother proceeded to say, "I have been wondering what would be the best way to pass out of this world without being a trouble to anyone, and the Lord has shown me that someday I shall lie down as usual to go to sleep and wake up in glory and this may be the last time that I shall see you; so now, my daughter, I feel constrained to urge you to seek the Lord." Again she said, "I am sure the Lord has shown me that I shall go that way." Four years later she went to glory just that way.

My parents had not given their hearts to God, yet they taught us to live right. The only religious services we ever attended were those held once a month in a country chapel. Other Sundays we would sing together in our home and father would read a sermon to us out of a book.

We would then repeat the Lord's prayer and sing another song.

One afternoon, when I was two and a half years old, a number of we children were invited to a neighbor's for lunch and play. As we passed the pantry window on our way in, we saw a number of dishes filled with nice red berries. One youngster suggested that we help ourselves to the berries, and this we did. After a few mouthfuls I began to scream and ran home. Mother, hearing my screams, rushed out to meet me and, picking me up in her arms, asked me where I was hurt. I couldn't tell her but kept screaming. Finally mother began to chide and shaking me, said, "Tell me where you are hurt." Still I could not speak, then mother fell upon her knees and cried, "Lord, my child is dying in my arms and I cannot find what is the matter with him." I was then able to speak and tell her the cause of my trouble. Putting my hand over my heart I said that I was having pain there and not in my stomach. Mother questioned me as to whether the lady had given us the berries, and I told her, "No," that we had helped ourselves to them. She said, "I will tell you how to get rid of your pain: Go and tell the lady what you have done and giving her your hand ask her to forgive you, and I am sure the pain will leave you." Mother went with me and when I confessed to the lady she took me up in her arms and wept with me. After confessing the pain all disappeared.

——— : : : : ———

When I was about eleven years of age it seemed that a voice was continually speaking to me and saying, "You ought to be a better boy; I want you for a preacher." I did not understand at the time that it was the Holy Ghost speaking to me. Mother often wept over me and said, "Child, O child, what shall I do with you! You make me more trouble than all the other eight children put together."

At the age of fifteen I was confirmed and at the following preaching service I was supposed to participate in taking the Lord's supper (as was the custom of the church). Before that service I went out into the woods to pray. I asked the Lord to forgive me for partaking of the Lord's supper, for to refrain from taking it would bring disgrace upon my family.

From that time on, the Lord continued to talk to me, saying, "You ought to be a better young man." It seemed as though I could not be better at home in Norway so I determined to sail for America.

I had been in America about a year and a half when I met a distant relative who was thought to be lost in this country, because his family had not heard from him for two or three years. He invited me to go into a saloon with him and have a glass of beer. We went in, and also played several games of pool.

In the meantime I took off my coat and hung it on the back of a chair. In the inside pocket of my coat I had my billfold containing about one hundred dollars, all the money I had, and also my valuable papers. When I went to reach for my money my billfold was gone. The saloon keeper seemed to know what had taken place and handed me five dollars. I had no work as there was none to be found. It was the custom in those days for the saloons to give a free lunch with a glass of beer. I went at noon every day and bought a glass of beer so I could have the free lunch that went with it. I lived that way for about two months.

During the late winter I got a job at night work, which consisted of pushing loads of stone in a wheelbarrow for the building of the Stone Arch Bridge over the St. Anthony Falls on the Mississippi River for the Great Northern Railway Company. The planks upon which we had to walk became very slippery and on one trip the man ahead of me slipped back in the wheel of my wheelbarrow upon which I had a large stone. The force of his fall threw both stone and wheelbarrow into the river. The man behind me, seeing what was happening, flung himself face down over his wheelbarrow, and in the dark, grabbed me as I was going over the plank into the river. He caught me by one of my arms and held me until help came and I was pulled out. I was hanging from his hands about fifty to seventy-five feet above the river.

After that experience I could not make myself walk those planks anymore, so I was again out of work and so terribly discouraged. A few nights later I walked onto the Tenth Avenue bridge intending to jump off into the river to end it all. As I took hold of the railing someone from behind me called out and said, "When you jump, your troubles will begin." I looked to see the man who had spoken but there was no one on the bridge. The way he spoke had sent a chill through me. It was after eleven o'clock at night and I seemed to realize that it was the Lord who had spoken to me.

After sometime in America I found that I was still the the same young man as before in Norway. It seemed that I was unable to do better. Thinking to improve matters, I decided to go to school and study for the ministry. After two semesters in the college certain things happened which turned me into an infidel. I quit school, went into business and got married. Soon after I contracted tuberculosis of the lungs, and the doctor said there was no help for me, as both my lungs were like soup. During the depression of 1892 I lost all I had. In my sinful condition I called on God and He healed me.

We then moved to the farm and one afternoon a young man came to our home and asked me to attend a service with him that evening. In answer to my query as to what kind of service it was to be, he informed me that two women evangelists were conducting the meeting. I replied that I was not in favor of women preachers but I would go with him as I was not afraid the women would hurt me. As a matter of fact, it was through these women that I was partly awakened spiritually, but did not yet give up my infidelity.

One evening I was very tired and sleepy and went to bed at precisely nine o'clock. I went to sleep at once and had a dream. I dreamed that I had become a minister of the gospel and that I was traveling all over the United States and Canada, as well as in a number of European countries. Hundreds of souls were turning to the Lord in the meetings and many healings and miracles were performed. It would take a long life to accomplish all that I saw done in my dream. I awakened and felt so refreshed and rested, that I thought it was morning and put on the light but found I had been in bed JUST TEN MINUTES! I did not sleep anymore that night but spent the time in meditating on my dream which convinced me that there must be within the human body a positive something that would continue to live forever and my infidelity vanished.

A few months later (March 12, 1895), the Lord spoke peace to my wife and me at the same time in our own home, and called us into the ministry. He brought us out of darkness through three visions and showed us the evil of all sectarian division. All this was giving us light on the beautiful Church of God without our having heard any preaching on the subject, nor did we know anyone who believed as we did.

We commenced preaching at once and our first convert

was a lady who was saved in our home. (Sister Hendricks, now Myhre, who is a minister). Our first case of healing was when the Lord healed me of blood poisoning in my left arm, caused from the scratch of a rusty nail. I caught cold in it and it swelled so fast that when I got into the house I could not get my clothes off and they had to be cut off with scissors. My wife and a young brother prayed for me, but I did not get immediate relief. My entire arm turned blue and yellow and soon my sides began to turn the same way. I had read in the Bible that the sick were to be anointed with oil. The young brother anointed me accordingly, and the swelling began to go down immediately, insomuch that the next morning there was no symptom of any thing wrong whatever.

———: : : : ———

The next experience of healing was of the restoring of my hearing to my right ear. My wife had gone to services and I stayed home to take care of the children. I had laid down beside them to get them to sleep and had dropped off to sleep myself, and dreamed that I saw Jesus standing beside the bed. He said to me, "Do you know John Pederson?" "Yes," I replied, "he is my neighbor." And Jesus said, "Isn't he a blacksmith and does he not make sleighs? And," he continued, "if he were to make one for you and you were to break it, wouldn't he fix it for you?" "Why, certainly," I replied. "Well," Jesus continued, "I made your ear in the first place and don't you think I can fix it?" "Yes," I said. Then He stepped up to me and touched my ear with two fingers and I jumped out of bed and MY HEARING WAS PERFECT! I shouted glory to God.

———: : : : ———

The youngest of our twin boys, who was nearly five years of age, was taken with double pneumonia and suddenly passed away. My mother-in-law prepared him for burial. As I was preparing to drive to town to get a permit from the doctor to bury the little one, the Lord said to me as I was on my way to the barn to get the team, "Why do you not go back and pray again?" I immediately turned around and went to the little corpse and laying my hands on him prayed and wept, and after a little while he came to life. He was not only alive, but also perfectly well. When I knelt down to pray my family did not dare to speak to me; they thought I had lost my mind.

About three years later our baby daughter, some ten months old, was sick and I was planning to leave home on Friday expecting to be gone over Sunday. The little one grew steadily worse and at eleven o'clock on Sunday night she passed away. There was great consternation in the family. The oldest boy fainted when his grandmother laid her out. After everything had quieted down and all had retired, except my wife who remained up, she went to the little body, held it in her arms as she knelt beside the bed until she was tired, then, laying the baby on the bed and laying her hands on it, prayed until life came back into it. When I returned Monday the child was as well as ever. In both cases grandmother prepared them for burial.

A little while after this experience the twins were out in the barn feeding the horses. Somehow in their actions one boy accidently stuck the tine of the pitchfork right into the eyeball of the other boy. Wife hearing their screams, ran out and brought them into the house. She washed the blood from the injured eye and laid the boy on the bed; then she and the twin brother laid their hands on him and prayed the prayer of faith. He went to sleep and slept untill morning, and all that remained on the eyeball was a small white spot in the center which disappeared after a day or two, and his sight was not in the least impaired.

———— : : : : ————

A similar case happened at Bruce, S. Dakota, while I was pastor at Brookings and White. The little three year old daughter of Brother and Sister Hi Tellinghuisen was playing in the yard with an old rusty sewing machine oil can. She fell on it, the spout striking right into the center of one eyeball. She was taken at once to a physician who ordered her to be taken without delay to a specialist to have the eyeball removed. The parents then called me over the telephone to come at once. When I arrived and saw the eye, it looked to me like a dried up prune stone. I anointed the child, but could find no words to utter in prayer. I could only groan, but the Lord witnessed to the healing. (I think this took place on Saturday at 11 o'clock a.m. and the next day, Sunday, she was brought to the services perfectly well. (At this writing she is teaching school).

———— : : : : ————

On March the 20th, 1904, wife was taken with quick consumption. Her fever was so high that she was delirious. As long as I remained beside her praying, she would be rational but as soon as I ceased praying her mind would wander. Over a week later, on Saturday, Brothers O. T. Ring and Carl Forsberg came to visit us. We then had agreement in prayer for the healing of my wife, and from that time on her mind was clear, yet she continued to go down. A number prayed for her but she grew weaker and weaker, until in the month of August. When the neighbors would come in to visit her, they would say to me on leaving, outside of the house, "We are sorry to say it, but we do not expect to see your wife alive again."

One day she said to me, "We have done everything we know to do except to send to Brother E. E. Byrum for an anointed handkerchief." I asked, "Do you want me to send for one?" to which she assented, and I sent for one. We received it by mail August the 23rd at 1 o'clock. I placed the handkerchief upon her and kneeling beside her laid my hands on her and prayed. She was so weak that it seemd as if she would pass away before I could remove my hands, so I soon said "Amen." She remarked, "This does not look very encouraging, does it?" I answered, "No, it does not." Then she drew one of her hands from under the covers and said, "Do you believe that any flesh is ever coming to these hands?" "Dear,' I answered, "I do not know." Then she said, "I believe that it will happen." I asked, "Why do you believe it?" She told me that a scripture had come to her while I was praying. She said that it was the one about Naaman: "His flesh came again like the flesh of a little child and he was clean." 2 Kings 5:14.

Two hours later she was perfectly well, but weak, of course.

———— : : : : ————

On one occasion I received an urgent call to come to Norway Lake to pray for Mrs. John Evenson who was ill with tuberculosis. While on my way there I battled with devils, it seemed as though my buggy was full of devils, whispering to me and saying, "You are going to be arrested and put in jail." However, after driving sixteen miles, the Lord assured me that He was going to raise Sister Everson up, even if she were dead when I got there.

As I drove into the driveway I saw a number of men

by the barn. It was the Constable and others. Jumping out of the buggy, I proceeded to unhook my team when Mr. Everson appeared, and said, "The hired man will take the team; come along with me." We went into the house and into the room where the sick woman was. Mr. Everson sat down in a chair beside the bed, taking his watch out, he then took his wife's hand in his to count the pulse. She was unconscious. I spoke to her two or three times but she did not hear me. I knelt down and asked the Lord to restore her to consciousness. Then I arose and spoke to her again. After a bit she opened her eyes and I said, "Brother Susag is here. What do you want him to do for you?" She replied, 'I want you to anoint me and pray for me." I immediately proceeded to do as she requested, following which she sat up in bed and asked for something to eat.

The constable, with others, was waiting outside the house to arrest me if the woman had died. Mr. Everson went out to them and they asked him how things were going. He told them that before I prayed for her, her pulse was 124, and when I took my hands off, her pulse was 82—which is normal!

Thirteen years later she was taken sick again. Mr. Everson, not being saved, called for the doctor they had previously employed. The doctor refused to come, saying that Mrs. Everson "had lived for thirteen years on something more than human. I can do nothing for her. If she has faith, she can live another thirteen years." Then they telephoned me. I drove two miles in my automobile and was taken seriously ill and had to return home and go to bed. I was very sick for two days. Mrs. Everson died in the meantime, and I was well.

On one occasion Brother C. H. Tubbs and myself held a meeting at Bowbells, N. Dakota and a number of people were saved. We were to have a baptismal service. It was the month of February and we would have to go three miles to the nearest lake in which to baptize the candidates There was no place there for the changing of clothes and it was slow traveling as we rode in a lumber wagon. Sister Stolsy, who wanted to be baptized, had been in poor health for five years and had a baby five weeks old. The Constable, on hearing of it, came to us and said, "If you put that woman through that hole in the ice, I'll be there with a warrant for your arrest." So Bro. Tubbs said, "We better go see Sister Stolsy," which we did. He said, "Sister, it does not look reasonable for you in your condition to be baptized." She wept and said, "I have wanted to be baptized for some time and now that I have the opportunity I am denied the privilege." Then I said to her, "Sister Stolsy, save your tears for something else. I will baptize you if I have to spend the remainder of my life behind the bars," and she was baptized. The constable witnessed the baptizing and saw that when she came out of the water she looked the very picture of health. Three days later the constable and his wife were baptized in the self-same place.

———— : : : : ————

I have baptized hundreds of people from Canada to San Antonio, Texas; from the Atlantic coast to the Pacific, in every month of the year, in the lakes of Norway, Sweden and Denmark as well as in the North Sea, in all kinds of weather—once in the Red River at Grand Forks, N. Dakota, in a snow storm in zero weather, and I have never yet heard of one person having taken cold from being baptized, but on the other hand, MANY HAVE BEEN HEALED!

It pays to obey the commandments of the Lord. While I was pastor in Grand Forks, N. Dak., from December, 1919 to November, 1925, I baptized over two hundred persons.

———— : : : : ————

Once in company with Thomas Nelson, C. H. Tubbs and my wife, we held a tent meeting in the country northwest of Colfax, Wisconsin. Several people were saved and some were healed. This stirred up great opposition so that on a couple of nights an angry mob was on the spot throwing stones, sticks and lumber and bottles on the tent, demanding that we come out and they would cut me to pieces. One night a minister of that community was in the tent, and as he saw the stones come rolling through the tent, he became badly frightened and said to me, "This is worse than in a heathen land." "Yes," I replied, "but are they not your people?" He said, "Yes," and then getting down on his hands and knees crawled out the back way from under the tent and escaped to the woods.

The reason for this unseemly tumult was because I had preached that baptism was by immersion and other truths. The situation was that two grown young people, the son and daughter of a minister in the community, were among those who were to be baptized. But the fact that there was no water nearby in which they could be immersed seemed to give the opposing element great satisfaction. However, we continued to advertise that there would be baptismal services on the coming Saturday afternoon. Friday night it rained heavily and near the tent there was a low place covered with green grass where the water settled and the water was deep enough in which to baptize the new converts.

This goes to prove that the Lord's resources are limitless. The next Sunday night, being the last night of the meeting, after all had left the tent except Bro. Tubbs and myself, and as I was not making any move towards leaving the tent Brother Tubbs asked me whether I was not going home. I answered, "No, those people who threatened to cut me to pieces are coming back to pull the tent down and I want to be here when they come, but you go on home; I want to be here alone." But he said, "No, I will not leave you."

It was about a hundred rods or more to the house where we were staying and there was no other house near by. We put out the lights and sat waiting. A number of times Bro. Tubbs urged that we go home, declaring that no one would come, but at almost midnight a plank was thrown on the tent and out ran Brother Tubbs for home; and then just as I was coming out of the tent a big plank was thrown on me, striking my right shoulder and also hit my head. It might have been quite serious but that I was wearing a stiff derby hat at the time. As it was, I was almost knocked out.

I said to them—there were between fifty and seventy of them, "Just a minute men, I am alone here; please do not destroy the tent; it has no feelings. Take me and cut me in pieces as you said you wanted to do. If I have done anything wrong I am willing to suffer for it." This I said as I walked slowly toward them, "But if it is because I have preached the Word of God to you folks and you do not receive it, you will meet it at the judgment bar of God," and I continued to walk toward them. They said, "Do not come so near." "Are you afraid of me?" I asked as I continued preaching to them. Then they commenced backing up. Finally, it seemed I had no more to say. One man said, "Give us more of that." At this point Brother Tubbs appeared with eight of the brethren, whereupon the crowd turned and ran for their rigs and vanished into the darkness.

About eighteen months later I held another meeting in this same community and the attendance was very good. A number of the same people who had claimed that they wanted to cut me to pieces were also there. Eight souls had gotten saved and the attendance was increasing. All of a sudden, as I was closing the service, the Spirit of the Lord said to me, "This is your last service here. You will leave in the morning on the 4 o'clock train for Grand Meadows, Minn." Saint and sinner alike, said, "You can't close now; look at the manifest interest and the growing attendance!" "But," I said, "the Lord tells me to close." They insisted that it could not be that they all were wrong and I the only one that was right. So I consented to stay, but had I but left on that morning train I would have escaped the terrible storm that swept over that part of the country. As it was, I could neither get away nor continue the meeting. On the farm where I was staying they had to have a rope extended between the house and the barn for two days in order to find the way from one building to the other.

———— : : : : ————

I had held a number of revivals for Brother Millar of Racine, Wisconsin. One time, in this connection, I had a dream that I saw a pasture with green grass and beautiful sparkling water running through it and as nice a flock of sheep as I ever saw were feeding in it. But in this beautiful pasture that should have been utilized for good pasture. I felt impressed to tell Bro. Millar of my experience so wrote him of what I had seen in my dream. In his prompt reply he said, "You had better come with your 'stump-pulling machine' and pull them out."

Some time later, on a very hot Sunday at noon I arrived in Racine, all tired and worked out. I asked Bro. Millar whether there was to be an afternoon service. I understood him to say, "No, there would not be." I said to him, "I want no lunch so please take me to my room." And this he did. I undressed immediately and was soon fast asleep, but before long I felt my bed being shaken and heard someone speaking to me but it seemed I just could not wake up. The shaking increased and I heard a voice saying, "Brother Susag, Brother Susag. I looked up and there was Brother Millar! He said, "Why, Brother Susag, have you undressed? The chapel is full of people who are waiting for you to come and preach." I told him I had understood him to say that there would be no afternoon service, that he should go back and that I would follow as quickly as possible.

I had no message. I opened my Bible and from Genesis to Revelation the Scriptures did not seem to mean anything to me. I prayed and still no message. Then coming down stairs I met Sister Anna Hanson who was just starting for the serivce. I said to her, "Please give me a text to preach on." She said, "O you will have a text." I told her I was in earnest, that I could not think of a single text in the whole Bible that meant anything to me, that I was too worn out to think. Sister Hanson then said, "I have often wished I might hear you preach on the first text I ever heard you preach on and that was in Chicago. The text was, "The Lord weigheth the spirits." Then the Lord opened my understanding and I had a text. At the close of the service Sister Hanson walked ahead of me to the parsonage and into the kitchen where Sister Millar was. She asked, "How was the service?" Sister Hanson answered, "The right message for the right people at the right time." Sister Millar said, "Well, praise the Lord!" and when Bro. Millar came in he said, "Praise the Lord," and jumped and shouted and said that every stump had been pulled—twenty-two of them!

While this meeting was in progress Brother Tiffany Flint from Milwaukee came down and asked me to come and hold a two weeks' meeting for him, but I had no open dates. In those days I was, at times, booked ahead as many as forty-two meetings, so I had to refuse him. But he urged, "Won't you come just a few days?" So I promised to go for three nights. When I arrived he said, "I have something to tell you: I have three persons here needing spiritual help." I replied, "Tell me nothing, on the train the Lord gave me three texts, one for each night, Tuesday, Wednesday and Thursday, which I am going to preach on." It happened that each text fitted each one of the three mentioned persons and each one came to service on the very night his particular text was preached on, and received his special benefit.

I am relating all these incidents because I have always believed in the leadership of the Holy Spirit; and now, after these fifty years of work in the ministry I am more firmly grounded in that belief than ever.

Some time later I held another meeting for Brother Millar. One afternoon, as I sat studying, the Lord said to me, "Here is your text; you go down to street so and so, such and such a number and preach at 2:30 this afternoon." After lunch I said to Brother Millar, "Let us take a walk." On coming out I said, "Is there a street in the city of such a name," stating the name the Lord had given me? He said, "I think so; what of it?" I told him that the Lord had given me a text to go down there and preach at 2:30. Bro. Millar then said, "We will take a street car and go down there and see, but I will tell you that if there is a chapel at that number you will not get an opportunity to preach there." We boarded the street car and the motor-man directed us to the street, and as we approached the given number we found a chapel and a meeting in progress. We went in and sat in the back seat. The singing had just stopped and the evangelist took his Bible and went to the pulpit. Bro. Millar smiled and hung his head, looking at me out of the corner of his eye, as much as to say, "I thought so." But I was pretty sober. I took my watch out of my pocket and held it in my hand and after the evangelist had given out his text and had spoken just seven minutes, he closed his Bible and said, "This is queer; I cannot speak this afternoon," and turning to the pastor, asked him whether he had the message. The pastor replied, "Why no, I haven't even my Bible with me." Then, looking over the audience, the evangelist said, "There must be someone here who has the message." Pointing to me, he said, "Haven't you got the message?" I answered, "Yes." "Then come on up here," he rejoined, "and take the pulpit."

On taking the pulpit I promptly explained just how it was we happened to be there at that particular time and proceeded to preach the sermon the Lord had given me to preach. I announced our services and everybody seemed to be well pleased with the sermon. I was not acquainted with any person in the audience, nor did any one know me as far as I knew. A little later a number of them attended our services and eight of them were saved and took their stand for the truth.

——— : : : : ———

At one time I received a series of letters from a leader in a certain Church of God congregation in which the writer earnestly pleaded that I come and hold a meeting for him.

He said that the Lord had revealed to him that I could be a great blessing to him and his congregation. I had never been to the place nor did I know anyone in the congregation that I was aware of. After giving the matter due consideration I felt that I should go, and wrote the pastor to that effect. On the day I was planning to leave I received a letter from the brother, upon the reading of which I began to tremble like a leaf—something I had never experienced before. I was standing on the floor reading the letter. Wife ran up to me and asked me if I was sick or whether there was anything wrong. She took the letter and read it, and said, "There is nothing wrong with that letter." "No," I said, "but I have a feeling that if I go I will meet something I have never met before." Wife answered, "Don't let the devil scare you now; you go, and I will pray for you."

On arriving in the city, as I stepped off the train, a man came up to me and said, "Are you Brother Susag? I am Brother X—; I have come to meet you. We certainly are glad that you have come, but I am sorry to have to tell you that our group is split into two congregations." I quickly reached to take my suitcase out of his hand, and said to him, "I'm going right back home; I'm too small a man to attempt to tackle anything like that." But he said, "No, you cannot go, for we have been praying for you to come and the Lord has shown us that you are the man to help us out." "All right," I said, "on one condition I'll stay. Take me to a hotel, and you inform both parties that I will only stay on condition that all meet together in one chapel and that no one tell me anything about the trouble, for if the Word of God will not make you one, I surely cannot do so." "But," said he, "you surely need to know something about how matters stand." "No," I replied, "the Lord knows it all and He also knows what messages to give me from time to time." "Very well," he said, "I'll take you out in the country three miles to an old couple who knows nothing of the trouble."

Three days later at three o'clock in the afternoon, the brother came to see me and informed me that my proposition had been accepted; the group had agreed to the conditions. I preached for eleven days and let them do their own altar work and the eleventh night there was but ONE congregation and all was peace and harmony. For the first eleven days of the meeting there was not one outsider in any of the services but on the very next night the chapel was filled, and there were seven ministers of the city present in the audience.

———— : : : : ————

An Assembly meeting was being planned, soon to be held in Chicago, at the 74th Street Church of God and the brethren in charge wrote to the ministers of the Scandinavian Publishing work in St. Paul Park, Minnesota, requesting them to provide an evangelist who should preach in the Scandinavian languages—either Thomas Nelson, Emil Krutz or S. O. Susag. Brother Krutz and I were holding a meeting at Hereford, Minn. at the time. We received a letter from St. Paul Park asking us to pray to find out which one of the three of us was to go. Then Brother Krutz said to me, "I know you know who is to go; tell me who it is." But I answered him, that he should go find out from the same source from which I had found out. He left me and after two hours returned and said, "It was a little hard for me to find out because I wanted to go so badly myself, but the Lord showed me that you were the one to go."

On my way I stopped at St. Paul Park and met Brother D. O. Teasley from New York. He said to me, "So you are on your way to the Assembly in Chicago." I said, "Yes, if Brother Nelson is not going." "Why," he said, "he is not going. When I stopped in Chicago the congregation was praying the Lord to send you." God works at both ends.

We held the Scandinavian services at the Assembly up stairs in the Missionary Home. After five days' meeting, quite a few were saved, while down in the English services in the chapel where there were thirty-three ministers, none were being saved. Brother Reardon, hearing of our good services, asked me whether I preached in English, "Yes," I replied, "in my broken way." "Why, then," he said, "do you not ask the Lord for a message to preach down in the chapel?" I answered, telling him the Lord had already given me three messages but someone else gets to the pulpit before me. (This was the time for the free-for-all in the pulpit). Brother Reardon said, "Come with me," and he took me upstairs into a room where a group of the leading ministers were assembled and said to them, "Here is the man who is holding up the success of the meeting." I said, "How is that possible when I cannot even get into the pulpit? Somebody rushes in ahead of me, and one who did so was not saved." To this they said, "We have already attended to that person," and told me that I had better get another message from the Lord, but I said, "No." Then they said, "Will you preach it if the Lord gives you another message?" I said, "I will, if I can get into the pulpit and you will pray for me."

The second day following, the Lord gave me another message. My text was the last clause of the second verse of Proverbs 16: " . . . the Lord weigheth the spirits." After I had spoken a few minutes Brother Cole spoke up and said, "Please stop a minute, Bro. Susag, do not talk so fast; we do not understand a word you say." I said, "Please pray for me." Then again, realizing I was going quite fast, I stopped when Sister Cole said, "Do not stop now, go ahead, Bro. Susag, we can understand you well enough." I seemed to be full of the Holy Ghost which seemed to be pressing me on. When I said, "Amen" there were forty-two at the altar crying for mercy.

Listen folks, this was not because of my good preaching, for they could not understand me, but they understood when the Holy Ghost spoke. When I went to the altar to pray with the seekers a man came running on his hands and feet, barking like a dog. He was taken out to another room to be prayed for. He was helped, and the devils were cast out.

After the altar service was over I asked Brothers Reardon and Ebel to go with me to the basement. As soon as we got there I fell on my face to the floor weeping, and saying to the brothers, "I need help, I am in serious trouble. It seems as though devils were tearing my very body to pieces." Thank God for good brothers who are able to help a person in time of need. Brother Reardon said to me, "Get up quick, Bro. Susag, don't lie there and cry for the devil." But I said, "You don't know what trouble I am in." But they said to me, "There is nothing the matter with you. Get up and rebuke the devil, get up and sit on that chair and we will talk to you." Then Bro. Reardon said, "The Lord used you to break the spell in the meeting and there were seven possessed with devils at the altar. The devil became enraged at you and was determined to ruin you." Then I resisted the devil and was free.

We will soon find out when we let the Holy Ghost have His way with us there are seemingly two equally great powers in the world. But thank God, we also find that He is the Omnipotent Ruler over all things.

Brother Tubbs and I once held a meeting at Portland, North Dakota. The wife of the man with whom we stayed professed to be saved and one of the saints. Her husband, as far as I knew, made no profession but was a very fine man and one of the leading business men of the town.

One day, as we were looking through the bookcase, we found a lot of fine looking books of Russellite teaching. We asked the sister who had bought them. She told us that she had bought them—"had bought over a hundred dollars' worth of those good books." We informed her that they were unsound, that they taught erroneous doctrine and should not be read nor handed to anyone.

Our taking this stand made things look as though we would be without a place to stay. But that evening the Lord changed the situation. The two-year-old child of this couple was suddenly taken violently ill. The mother asked us to pray for the boy. Bro. Tubbs plainly told her that the Lord would not heal her boy as long as she had those books in the house. When we were just starting to go to the service that evening, the father, who was holding the child in a blanket in his arms, said to us, "Will you guarantee healing to my child if I place it in your hands? Otherwise I shall have to get a doctor before it is too late." Bro. Tubbs answered, "We can guarantee nothing,' and we started for the service.

Bro. Tubbs was already outside the door of the house when the mother of the child said pleadingly, "Won't you pray?" The Holy Ghost came upon me and I said, "Yes, on one condition, if you will promise to take all those books over to the meeting place tomorrow and burn them up before the eyes of the audience, I'll pray and guarantee healing for your child." She said, "I won't do that; they are good books and cost $100." "All right," I said, and stepped out of the door. The father said, "Just a minute," and then to his wife he said, "Isn't the life of our child worth more than one hundred dollars?" She said, "But they are good books." He replied, "The ministers say they are no good. I know nothing about them, whether they are good or not, but I do know one thing that my child's life is worth more than one hundred dollars." "All right, then, I'll do it," she said.

I stepped back in the room, threw my hat on the floor, went over and laid my hands on the child and prayed the prayer of faith and the Lord healed the child instantly, and the books went up in smoke the next day.

I have seen bookcases and book shelves in many homes that need just such a purge in order that the glory of God may dwell in the home, and sometimes even in the churches.

——— : : : : ———

In the years 1915-16 I spent almost thirteen months in Denmark helping the few faithful workers there to raise up eight congregations and many books were burned during the time.

One old mother in Israel, when she heard of the books being burned, said, "I've got only one book and it's a good one." She brought it to me and said, "If you say this is not good, my salvation goes too." I asked her if I might mark with a pencil in her book and she said I could. After reading it a while I laid it aside having marked it here and there. She asked me what I thought of her book. Not to discourage her, I said, "There are some good things in that book." She took it and began to find the places which I had marked, finally closed the book and said, "This book is no good; the Bible says thus and so and the book speaks to the contrary." Then she said, "Why have I been blessed many times when reading this book?" I answered, "Because you were honest and did not know any better."

We pioneer ministers had many things to meet. On getting home one time, I found that a runaway team had pulled our windmill down so that we had to have a new one. The well was 204 feet and was hard to pump. After we got the new one, a neighbor came over and said to my son, Oswald, "See, your father has been out preaching and so you are able to have a new windmill." Yes, he had been gone seven weeks and he was eleven cents short on his expenses. The following year I was gone nine months and five days and I fared real well—I had $76.76 above my expenses that time.

———: : : :———

Sometimes I got to thinking about little Charlie Brown, who I believe was about eleven years old at the time. When his father asked him if he got tired, he said, "Yes, I get tired of this walking preaching." So they went into a grove and prayed and his father said to him, "We will go to the next town and you preach on some street corner and if no one gets saved, we will quit and if some get saved we will keep on. What do you think of that?" Young Charlie agreed to that and a number of souls did get saved. Now "young Charlie" is Editor in Chief of the Gospel Trumpet.

Then it was empty pocketbooks, empty stomachs and sore feet, but that did not stop the preaching. Yes, in those days it was SOULS we were after, and not money and honor.

———: : : :———

I did not have a new suit for sixteen years; wife had only one new dress in eighteen years. Although we lived on a farm we could not eat butter. We had to sell that in order to be able to buy more necessary things.

One year wife and the children were raising twenty-two hogs while I was out preaching in the gospel field, and we had a payment of $500 to make on our home, or move. When I arrived home in the fall wife met me with tears in her eyes as she told me that the hogs were all ready for the market when the price dropped from $6:00 per hundred weight to $2.75. "And," she continued, "the only reason I can find for it is that we have not given enough." "But," I replied, "I feel that we have given enough: Our gross income has been a little over $500.00." She then brought two pencils and two pieces of paper and said to me, "Come on." We knelt down and asked the Lord to bring to our minds what we had given, and in our check-up we found we had given $252.50. Then, almost scaring me, my wife, with tears streaming down her face, lifted her hand toward heaven, and said, "Lord, we have done our duty and you will have to pay our bills."

Two days later the cattle buyer came back and said that if he could get our hogs he would have enough for two railroad carloads. I told him he could not have them at that price. He said, "They are the nicest looking hogs I ever saw and if I can get them to mix in with the others I may get top price for all." "And," he added, "I will give you the old price: Six dollars ($6.00) per hundred weight." To which I replied, "They are yours."

One of our neighbors had twenty-two hogs born the same week as ours. The day they were brought into town people said, "Susag's hogs are the nicest, but P—'s hogs will weigh 1,000 pounds more than his." They weighed them and found that our hogs weighed almost eleven hundred pounds more than P—'s. They took them off the scales twice to examine the scales to see whether they were correct, but the hogs held their weight, almost eleven hundred pounds more than the neighbor's hogs. So once more, the Lord honored his faithful, humble people. There was enough money for the $500 payment and some to spare.

Two years later we had another $500 payment to meet, and when we started to seed in the spring, I said to the twins, "Let us kneel down right here in the field and ask God to give us a large enough crop to pay the notes which will be due in the fall." That year crops, generally, were very poor, average wheat being from 2½ to 3½ bushels to the acre (of screenings, or Number Four, as it is called). But the Lord gave us eighteen bushels to the acre on one piece and on the other, twenty-two bushels to the acre of Number One wheat. One old lady said, "I can't understand such a thing—only a fence between."

——— : : : : ———

One time I had a dream of a scene taking place in the chapel at St. Paul Park, Minn. Brother Nelson, who had just finished his sermon, was standing by the pulpit with his left elbow on the pulpit and his hand on his chin, looking at the audience. Then I saw a woman, about two-thirds down the aisle, get up and shake her fist toward Bro. Nelson. The Lord said to me, "Do you see that woman?" I answered, "Yes." "You see she is not right with me in shaking her fist at my servant?" "Yes," I said, "I can see that." Then the scene changed in my dream. I was sitting on a chair right between the dining room and the front room at the Workers' Home of the Scandinavian Publishing Company, and there was a minister sitting behind me leaning his hands on the back of my chair. This minister I had met once before, and the Lord said to me, "You had better look out for that man; he is not right with me. He will get you into trouble."

Personal Experiences of S. O. Susag

Some days later I received a telephone message to come to St. Paul Park, Minn. at once. I went accordingly. On my arrival I found services were going on in the Workers' Home and very soon I was sitting exactly as I saw myself sitting in my dream. All of a sudden I saw the woman I had seen in my dream coming in from the kitchen. I had never seen her before, nor had I ever heard of her, but recognized her from the dream. Then I almost got scared. What if that preacher was sitting behind me resting his hands on the back of my chair, I thought. What's up, anyhow? I did not dare to look back to see!

The brethren asked me to preach, and when I got up and faced the audience, sure enough, there sat the very minister I had seen in my dream! I spoke on the twenty-third Psalm. I'm generally long winded in the pulpit but this time I cut it short. When I closed, Bro. Nelson said, "Is that all you are going to give us?" And I said, "Yes."

"Old men shall have dreams and young men shall see visions."

When the service was over, Brother O. T. Ring came to me and said, "Please come into our room; we want to see you a little." On going into the room I found that the ministry were there, along with this minister and woman, also some of the leading workers. Brother Nelson said, "We are having a little difficulty and we felt that we should call for you. You have had a lot of experience and we thought that possibly you could be a help to us." Then I got up and asked whether I might tell my dream. After I had told it I said, "If this fits, then you let me out." "Yes, it fits," he said.

A number of years later Brother J. S. Lane was to be the evangelist at the South Dakota State Camp Meeting. We met and introduced ourselves. Brother Lane said,

"Brother Susag, I stopped at Clinton, Iowa, and a sister said to me, are you going up to South Dakota and Minnesota? Then you'll meet a minister that I am afraid of. His name is Susag; the Lord speaks to him whether he is asleep or awake, but I have forgotten her name." I said, her name is so and so. "Yes," he said. That was about twenty years after the dream.

———— : : : : ————

It was a wonderful experience the Lord gave me after the baptism of Sister Swenvorg and the wonderful healing of her eyes, and also the wonderful glory the Lord sent upon her with the persecution that came with it. That evening in the service the Lord blessed me so much I had to put both hands over my heart and had to ask the Lord to stop, as my human body could not stand any more pressure. This happened in Lukken, Denmark.

———— : : : : ————

I once went to hold a meeting in Bro. William Gustafson's grove three miles north of Belgrade, Minnesota. The brother met me at the station and said he had quite a lot of business to do in town so I could stay at that station until he got through and then he would come and get me. But as quite a long time passed and he did not come I walked over to a store and asked them if they knew Mr. Gustafson and they said they did. Then I asked if they knew whether he was still in town. To which they replied that he had gone home quite a while ago. So I had to take my grips and walk out to his place, as the meeting was set and I was to stay in his home. I held the meeting and some souls were saved, but I never said a word to Mr. Gustafson about his leaving me in town. I thought that the good Lord could speak to him better than I could. The Lord gave me grace to treat him as nicely as though nothing had happened. When the meeting ended I had to walk back to town again.

At the next year's state camp meeting he came to me and said, "Can we go over into the timber?" Of course I said, "Yes." On our way over he told me that a would-be preacher had talked to him about me, accusing me of many things but that he had found out that they were not true. Then he asked me to forgive him and he also asked the Lord to forgive him, as he had lied to me.

It is too bad that such things happen, as a finer brother than Brother Gustafson there never was.

Then Brother Gustafson told me that the Lord spoke to him telling him he should have given ten dollars to me for that meeting, but now the Lord tells him it is to be fifty, and he wrote me out a check for that amount.

―――― : : : : ――――

A WONDERFUL INCIDENT

Father Brewster, as he was commonly called, of Hereford, Minnesota, was taken sick and was sick for some time. If I am correctly informed, he was 89 years of age. For a number of days it was thought that he was dead but the doctor said that he was still living, but he might go almost any time, and the family sent for me to come and conduct the funeral services. He had been in a coma for eight days. On arriving I found that the doctors had not yet pronounced him dead. I went into the bedroom where he lay and stood looking at him for a few minutes, meditating on the many good times we had had together in the Lord. Finally I fell on my knees and began to pray. Suddenly he called out in a loud voice, "Praise the Lord, Brother Susag." He never moved a hand or a finger, all that he moved was his lips and the next day he passed away. He had not spoken a word for eight days.

———— : : : : ————

One year when I was the evangelist at the S. Dakota State camp meeting, I mentioned one day in my sermon that I was very busy and had received enough calls since I had come to the camp meeting to keep me going for two years. After the service Brother Geselbeck, the elder of the church, came to me and said, "Let us go down to the car," which we did. He began by saying, "I've always had confidence in you, Brother Susag, but today in something you said, I thought you went too far, so I decided to speak to you at once as I did not want to lose my confidence in you." I said, "Thank you, that's fine, brother; what was it I said?" "You said that you had received enough calls since you had been at the meeting to keep you going for two years, and this is only the third day!" "Did I say that?" I asked. "Maybe I said too much, but we will see. I have the letters here in my pocket and they are addressed to Arlington, Route 1, South Dakota." So we took the letters and read them and found that if I were to hold meetings at each place as long as they stated in the letters it would have taken me twenty-six months. Bro. Geselbeck then said, "I knew you were a busy man, but I never knew you were that busy, and I am glad that I spoke to you!" Yes, if we would all do that way when something is in question it would avoid a whole lot of misunderstanding.

———— : : : : ————

I once had a cancer on my upper lip and one day I met Dr. Sandven on the street of my home town. He stopped and said to me, "You had better come over to the hospital and we will burn that thing out or else you WILL have something." I replied, "I've got something already." "Yes," he said, "but we may be able to burn it out yet." "Well," I said, "I believe I will wait on my own Doctor a little while yet." "All right," he said, "if you don't get rid of it, come over and we will try to help you."

A few days after this I went to Erie, North Dakota to hold a tent meeting for Sister Bertha Gaulke who was the pastor of the church there. We had prayer often, but for two nights the pain was so intense it seemed as though the roots of the cancer were going into my nose and up into my left eye. The third night I was weeping and praying and finally I went to sleep, and in my sleep the Lord said to me, "Wake up and take hold of the cancer; I have heard your prayers and it will come out." I woke up and did as the Lord directed, and out it came, roots and all!

I have had (and still do have) many dreams. The Bible says, that " . . . old men shall dream dreams, your young men shall see visions." (Joel 2:28).

———— : : : : ————

During the time I was pastor in Grand Forks I needed a fountain pen. Sisters Hulda and Louise Werstlein gave me five dollars to get a pen, to be my Christmas present. I sent to my son, who was agent for such things, and he got me a $7.50 Waterman pen for the five dollars. After the Minnesota State camp meeting, Sister Moon of Canbee, Minnesota asked me to take her and her two children home. On reaching Montevideo I met Brother Thomas Nelson who said he would like to have a long talk with me. I told him that he could take Sister Moon and the children and myself and we could talk then as we went back and forth, which we did, but when I arrived home my pen was gone!

I wrote to the pastor at Montevideo asking him to look in Brother Nelson's car and around in the grass where the car had stood, thinking the pen might have fallen out of his car when I took my coat out of his car and put in in mine. About a week later I got a card saying there was no pen to be found anywhere.

A few nights later I had a dream. I saw my pen. It was standing up against a small willow in a bunch of grass in the road ditch; it was very dusty.

Some days after this, as I was on my way to town going north, I passed the road going west which I had been on when I lost my pen. The Lord said, "Why don't you go and get your pen?" I laughed to myself, but kept on driving and again the Lord said, "Why don't you get your pen; why don't you get your pen?" Finally I had to turn back, and as I did so I said to myself, "This is a trip that I'll never tell anyone about, starting out for 136 miles to look for a pen in a road ditch!"

After going a mile and three quarters I saw to my left a little willow sticking up just like the one I saw in my dream. I stopped the car and went to look, and there stood my pen just as it was in my dream.

We might ask how it got there. The only answer I can give is that I must have had my coat over the front seat of the car and the coat must have fallen down, and when I reached for it while the car was going the pen must have fallen out of my coat pocket in the dark.

——— : : : : ———

A WONDERFUL INCIDENT

I had arrived home on Saturday, and Sunday I went to the service. The pastor said, "Now I know why I haven't a message today," and turning to me he said, "You speak for me." But I said, "No, I did not bring my Bible along." "Well," someone said, "we can let you have a Bible." I said, "Soneone else must have the message." There were two other ministers there, but neither had a message. Finally wife said, "Husband, I get a number of letters and here's one that reads like this, 'Dear Sister Susag: You should have been in our service last night. We had a wonderful message and a wonderful service. Several were saved, and do you know who preached for us? Your husband preached for us.'" Then she said, "Why don't you give us a message like that at home?" And they all said, "That's right."

Then I got a text. I looked at my watch and it was eleven o'clock. I knew the pastor had to be home at 12:30, but I forgot all about it, and not a person moved, not even the little children, while I preached. When I quit I thought it would be around 12:10 or 12:15, but on looking at my watch it was 3:15 in the afternoon. I had preached for four hours and fifteen minutes and the pastor and audience declared there must be something wrong with our watches! It seemed as if we must have been pretty close to the third heaven!

———— : : : : ————

On one occasion while I was in Europe I visited at my wife's request, a cousin of hers who had been ill and confined to her bed for twenty-one years. She had become bedfast when she was nineteen. When I first visited her, as she did not understand anything about divine healing, she got quite peeved at the instructions I gave her. However her father, my wife's uncle, got gloriously saved. Two weeks later I got a letter from the woman asking me to come again and I went. Then she repented and turned to the Lord. I prayed for her and the Lord raised her up.

———— : : : : ————

Once in a city called Stavanger, Norway, I was asked to come and pray for a sister who was in the last stages of tuberculosis of the lungs. As some of the people over there teach that it is witchcraft to heal by the word of God and prayer, a mob had gathered to stone me, and the folks called me and asked me not to anoint and pray for fear the people might do me bodily harm. I told them that I was not any better than the apostles or any other of God's ministers, and if that was to be my lot I would be willing to die for the gospel's sake.

I anointed and prayed for the woman and the Lord raised her up to the great astonishment of the people and no bodily harm came to me.

I met her twin sister several years later who said she had been well ever since, healthy and strong.

———— : : : : ————

In 1916 while in Denmark I contracted tuberculosis of the throat and head. I got so weak that while holding a meeting in company with Brother Carl Forsberg out from Pandrup, Denmark, one evening before the service started I was suffering so intensely that I went out into the cow barn, sat down on a milk stool coughing and spitting, praying and weeping until I was so weak that I was unable to get up when I tried to do so. Time for meeting came, and the folks did not know what had become of me, so a Brother Madson, a big strong man, went out to look for me. When he found me he picked me up and carried me in, laid me on the lounge and the saints prayed for me, and I got strength to get up and preach. We closed the services that evening. Brother Forsberg returned to Sweden and I to my headquarters at Hjoring. I went to a specialist and asked him to write me a permit so that I could return to America. After he had examined me he said that he could not give me the permit as I would not be permitted to go aboard ship in the condition I was in. He said, "You would not live until you got there if you did start." I told him that I would like to be with my folks when I leave this world. He replied, "I don't blame you but it can't be done."

Then I got a letter from Brother and Sister Johnson of Jotta, Sweden, saying that "Brother Forsberg had come home saying that it looked as though the Lord was through with Brother Susag, he was no near gone. Wife and I agreed in prayer and the Lord says He is going to heal you and that you are going to preach to us here many times."

The following Sunday we had services in Hjoring at eleven o'clock, although I did not seem to be able to stand up, but I thought I might just as well go to heaven from the pulpit as to go from the bed, if I was going to die anyway. After I had been speaking about fifteen minutes I quit, as the pain got so intense in my throat I could hardly speak above a whisper, and the audience could not hear me. I went up stairs in the chapel where I had my room, and I lay down on the bed suffering intensely.

Outside my door was a tree and a little bird hopped onto a branch and began to sing. (I do not know the name of the bird, but the species was like the birds that used to come to our grove at home in Minnesota and sing. But I had never before heard one in my travels in Europe). I turned to the bird and said, "Did my heavenly Father send you from Minnesota to Denmark to sing for me when I was so troubled?" And the more I would speak to him the more he would flap his wings and sing and sing until I could forget my pain and had to laugh aloud. It was nearly four o'clock and that was the time for the next service. I got up and got ready for the service, and when I came into the pulpit to preach, to my surprise, I was perfectly healed and could speak as loud as ever without pain.

The next morning I went to the specialist and asked him to examine me again to see if I could go home if I wanted to. After examining me he said, "Man, O man, what have you done? There is not a T. B. germ about you— you can go or stay as you please." I told him I had done nothing, but that the people of God had been praying for me, the results of which was a great surprise to the doctor. This is the way the Lord deals with his unworthy, humble children that trust and obey Him.

———— : : : : ————

I have generally observed a rule of not eating my evening meal until after the evening service. One evening in Sweden I ate a little fish out of a can that had been standing open for some time. After eating a little of the fish I remembered that the can had been standing open and did not eat any more. About a half an hour after I had retired and gone to sleep, I woke up feeling deathly sick with ptomaine poisoning. It seemed as if I was to be taken out of this world. All through the night Brother Forsberg, Sister Bettie Miller and others kept praying for me and the next day my life seemed to hang on a thread, but at five o'clock that evening we got the victory and I was perfectly healed, and able to speak in the service that night.

Some years afterwards while at Camp meeting at Anderson, Ind. I was poisoned in about the same manner. A number of brethren prayed for me without my getting any relief. Finally, Brother George Green, now pastor at Hanford, California, a true yoke-fellow of mine who loved me dearly, broke down and wept and had compassion on me and prayed a short prayer of faith and rebuked the devil and the sickness, and I was healed instantly. The Bible says of Jesus, "He had compassion on the people and healed all that came unto him."

———— : : : : ————

On one ocassion in 1933 I was not feeling very well. I was on my way to California and stopped in Minneapolis where my three boys live. When they saw that I was not well, they were determined to take me to a doctor and have me examined. He ordered me to a hospital where five doctors took six x-rays. After taking the x-rays, the doctors asked me, "What do you think you have?" I said, "The same as you think." They said, "What do we think?" "Cancer!" I said. "No," they said. I said, "Why do you lie, you said it was cancer and a bad one." They said, "Do you understand Latin?" I said, "I understand that much." In the evening the doctor called my son Clarence and said to him, "Shall I tell your dad what the matter is with him, or will you?" He answered, "It doesn't matter who tells him, as he is ready to live or to die; we want to know the worst." The doctor said, "It is the worst. Bring him to my office tomorrow at three o'clock." I heard the five doctors talking the case over between themselves, stating the position of the cancer.

On coming to the office the next day the doctor said, "I have good news for you, Reverend, you have no cancer." I asked him, "When did you lie to me, yesterday or today?" He said, "Neither, the picture clearly shows cancer. They forgot to take your food test so you had to go back to the hospital to have it taken and in the food test there was no cancer." The doctor asked, "What did you do, once a cancer but none now?" I said, "I did like a little story we ministers have about a little boy and his sister. They were out playing, and at eleven o'clock Mary was hungry and went in to ask mother for a slice of bread, but mother said, it is soon time for lunch, go out and play now, until lunch is ready. Then Freddy went in and asked for bread and he came out with a slice of bread with butter on it. Then Mary said, 'What did you do to get it?' 'I cried for it,' answered Freddy," so did I.

The Lord made them forget to take the food test at first in order to verify the miracle.

———— : : : : ————

One day I was plowing, since I had asked the boys to let me plow for the exercise it gave me. It was about ten o'clock in the morning and I had stopped and gotten off the gang plow to let the horses rest and stood looking south in the field when I saw six or eight feet before me dear Brother A. G. Ahrendt standing and smiling at me, just as real as if he were there in the flesh. "Brother Ahrendt is leaving Grand Forks by my orders," the Lord said to me. "If by your orders he is leaving there, amen," I replied. I then turned to get on the plow when on the other side of the plow there stood a lady minister and the Lord said, "Some are contemplating getting her as the pastor and that will be the ruination of the work in Grand Forks." (Not because there was anything wrong with her as a minister but because she would not fit in the place). The vision disappeared and I went to plowing.

Two or three days later I became so burdened about Grand Forks that I was almost sick, so I wrote to Brother

Ahrendt and asked if anything was wrong or anyone sick, for I was so burdened. I expected an answer right away, but didn't get it, so wrote again and still no answer. The next week I wrote for the third time telling them that I was going through Grand Forks on my way to Raab for a meeting, and would be in Grand Forks and they could arrange a meeting for me over Friday night, Saturday and Sunday if he wanted me. Then a letter came from Sister Ahrendt saying her husband was away and that they were leaving Grand Forks.

Sunday afternoon, when in Grand Forks, I went by invitation to Brother Lars Olson's home and there met the four leaders of the congregation: August Shave, Bertha Gaulke, Lars Olson and Sister Johnstone. They told me that they had been talking of sending for me; Bro. Shave had proposed sending me the money for carfare, but Bro. Olson said, "No, we won't do that; we will ask the Lord to send him here and we will pay his expenses when he comes." These prayers going up from the dear ones in Grand Forks was what made the Lord burden my heart before I went there.

They then begged me to be their pastor, and I finally consented to come and stay with them for a month or three months or until they could get a pastor. I stayed with them for almost five years.

———— : : : : ————

While holding a meeting in company with Brother Renbeck in a school house out in the country between Kelly and Manville, N. Dakota and staying in the home of Bro. and Sister Holman, one afternoon as I was praying the Lord gave me a message on the JUDGMENTS OF GOD, and what would happen, even in this world, if people reject the Word of God. The Lord said to me, "They will close the school house." Then I asked Brother Holman if we should close the services tonight, where shall we go if we continue them? He said, "We surely are not going to close the services tonight; we will continue at the school house." I said, "The school house will be closed to us tonight." To which he answered, "Who said so?" I told him that the Lord had told me. Brother Holman then said, "You are a good Brother, but this time you are mistaken, for they would not dare close the school house because three of the saints' families are the biggest taxpayers in the district."

At the beginning of the service that evening, Brother Renbeck got up and commenced to preach on the subject, "The Church as a House." After speaking for about ten minutes, he sat down and said, "This is not the message for tonight." We knelt down and prayed asking the Lord to give a message, and the Lord said, "I have given you a message." I said, "Lord, that is too strong," but the Lord answered, "It is the message for this people."

The school house was large and it was filled. It was said that there were two or three congressmen in the crowd. I got up and spoke for an hour and fifteen minutes on the message the Lord had given me and when I was through I said, "Shall we close the services now, or has anyone a place to offer so we can continue the meeting, as I understand that the school house is closed against us?" The clerk of the school board (who with his family were professors of religion) went over to Bro. Holman and asked him who had told Susag that the school house was to be closed. The Board had only met just before meeting and decided to close. Brother Holman replied that Brother Susag told him that afternoon that the Lord had told him that they were going to close. The man went back to his seat. Then I said, "Is it true or not that the school house is to be closed?" Brother Holman answered, "It is true."

One man in the audience sat on the front edge of the bench so deeply interested in the service that his mouth would be wide open, and after the meeting was over he stuck a five dollar bill in my hand and said that the meeting had been worth that to him.

A man in the audience, who was an infidel, said, "I own a store building in Mechinoch, a few miles away, that these two preachers may have as long as they please, if some one can furnish a stove and wood to warm up the building." The stove and wood were promptly furnished, and we went there accordingly, and continued our services.

I am sorry to say that many who heard the Word of God preached in that school house rejected it and became real outlaws. The family of the school board clerk lost their salvation and two of their sons, who had previously professed salvation, became bootleggers.

At the store building a number of people got saved. One man sat in the back seat every evening and left as soon as the preaching was over. I saw that he was under conviction and one evening I got to him before he had left, and I asked him if he did not want to get saved and he told me, "Yes." While praying with him I felt a hand on my shoulder and a man said to me, "Brother Susag, Brother Susag, never mind this man; there are thirty-three at the altar and this man has not been sober in fourteen years." I said, "If he has not been sober for fourteen years he surely needs salvation and I will stay with him until he gets saved." And I did; and as far as I know he remained a true Christian and lived the life.

The first revival meeting we ever had in our neighborhood was held in our own house. The house 16 x 24, two rooms down stairs and one room upstairs. As many as thirty-eight slept in the house; the women and children slept upstairs and the men downstairs. There was one bed in which the children slept and the women slept on the floor as did the men downstairs. People were saved, sanctified and healed. It was salvation the people wanted in those days.

—— : : : : ——

Our first camp meeting was held in a tent a mile and three-quarters from our home. Warning was sent around the neighborhood for the people to lock their chicken coops as the camp meeting was being financed only by two poor men, who were giving free meals to all who came.

We had a wonderful meeting; many souls were saved and sanctified and devils were cast out, some were healed. We had some very straight preaching as we had some very fiery ministers who preached, such as, Brother and Sister C. M. Tubbs and the Brothers Enos and Elihu Key, Brother Thomas Nelson and Brother Tilgut.

The country around was stirred and people tried everything in their power to hinder the meeting. Some businessmen of our own home town (Paynesville) hired a team and borrowed a three or four-seated platform buggy from the implement Company and placed a small cannon on it, drove to within a few rods of the gospel tent and fired the cannon. The chairman of the town Board came to me and wanted me to have them arrested. But I said, "No, let them go."

The Lord "fined" them for us: As they were shooting off the cannon the horses took fright and ran away into the timber, smashing up the new buggy and tearing the harness to pieces. That saved us the court proceedings.

———— : : : : ————

The second camp meeting I was in, among the saints, was at Grand Forks, N. Dakota. I was called there especially to preach in the Scandinavian language as well as to help in the English preaching. When the first evening service was over every one who had no place to sleep was to stand outside the tabernacle near the big oak tree. One by one they got their place to sleep. Finally I was left standing all alone in the dark. No one offered me a place so I walked around among the trees. The camp meeting was held in the timber along the banks of the Red River. While I was looking for a place to lie down and rest, a man came running toward me and said, "Don't you have a place to sleep?" I said, "No." He said, "You go to that covered wagon over there and you'll find a place." As I approached the wagon I saw six feet sticking out of the wagon, almost to the knees, so there was no room for me.

I went back to the tent and shoved three or four planks together. These planks had been used for seats. I put my suit case down for a pillow and there I slept that night and during the rest of the meeting. When I would get a little cold in the night I would get up and walk around a bit. A few days later Oluf Erickson from Belgrade, Minnesota, who had gotten saved in one of our meetings at home, asked me where I was sleeping. I said, "I have a good place; another brother and I have a very fine tent with a bed in it." "Oh yes," he said, "I know where you sleep; you sleep in the minister's tent." "Yes," I said, "it's a minister's tent all right." But he didn't give up until he found out the truth. He then said, "My, my, had no one offered you a place to stay, and you are one of the evangelists?" I said, "Yes." Then he said, "Well then, I'll come and sleep with you."

In those days it was: "All for Jesus and souls" and not for personal comfort. We had a wonderful time together in the Lord. We also had a wonderful camp meeting in seeing scores of souls saved and many miracles done by the power of God.

Sister Renbeck, who had been bed fast for a long time, was carried in on a cot and the prayer of faith was offered. Brother E. E. Byrum took her by the hand and commanded her to arise in the name of Jesus. She arose and went running around the tent lifting her hands and praising God. I heard three men talking about it afterwards saying, "I wonder if that is real! She surely looked poorly and puny, but you can't tell." Another man said, "I wish my wife had been here; if it had been HER we would have known it was real." (She had been sick for a long while.)

―――― : : : : ――――

While my first meeting in Grand Forks was in progress, Brother Renbeck came to me with the request that I would pray over a matter he had on his mind, and that was that after the meeting was over he and I might go together to hold a meeting at Whitten, Minnesota. I promised to pray over the matter and that at the close of the meeting we would talk it over together. And, accordingly, at the end of the meeting I prayed earnestly to get the mind of the Lord as to where He wanted me to go.

When Brother Renbeck asked me what I had gotten from the Lord in regard to the matter I replied by asking whether there were places in North Dakota by names of Kelly, Grafton and St. Thomas, "Yes," he said, "there are; what of it?" I replied that the Lord told me I was going to those places. He told me that just before the meeting here, he had come from those very places and there would be no use in going. I told him I was going to follow the leading of the Lord and go, that he could stay here until I came back when we would go to Whitten. But he declared if I was going he would go, too.

That trip proved to be the beginning of a wonderful work of God. Many people were saved and many healings and miracles were wrought by the Spirit of the Lord. In our visiting, the first house we entered at eleven A.M. an elderly sister, ninety years of age, was sanctified and her husband, ninety-three years old, was saved before twelve o'clock that day. This shows that Brother Renbeck had laid a good foundation in these places, preparing the way for the wonderful evangelistic trips that followed. Neither of us ever went to Whitten.

While at Grafton, N. Dakota, Brother Renbeck and I had the experience of holding a number of meetings in private homes. Interest increased and so did our problems.

One day we wanted to telephone to Brother C. H. Tubbs at Grand Forks. We went to a telephone office and were told that the cost of a message would be twenty-five cents. We counted up our change and between us found that we had only twenty-four cents, and so we had to leave the office disappointed. Out on the side walk we stood facing each other, one of us said, "Wasn't it too bad that we didn't have another penny?" I was standing with my back to the street when I heard the Lord say to me, "Turn around, a penny is lying right behind you." I turned around and there it was. I picked it up and we sent the message, but Brother Tubbs was not at home.

There was an old retired Methodist minister attending our meetings right along, declaring that divine healing died away with the departure of the Apostles. The next Sunday seven women were saved, one of whom was a young lady which had a stiff arm and crooked to such an extent that she could neither dress nor undress herself without assistance. She was prayed for and I asked her if she believed that the Lord would straighten out her arm and she replied, "Yes," but did not move it. I happened to be looking at the old minister and it seemed to be written all over his face: "Just as I expected." At the beginning of the evening service we gave opportunity for testimony and this young lady was all on fire to testify. She said, "I love Jesus and Jesus loves me, and He makes my arm well;" and then she raised her arm and waved it in all directions. The old minister bowed his head to his knees.

The next day we were called to the home of a young lady who was suffering from inflamatory rheumatism. Her entire body was stiff; her legs were crossed below her knees and her arms were crossed over her breast and were immovable, except that she could move her hands slightly and also her head a little. The doctor was coming twice every day to give her a morphine injection to ease the pain or she would make a disturbance by screaming at the top of her voice.

When we first visited her, Brother Renbeck began immediately to talk to her about salvation, for he thought that she must be saved before she could be healed. However, we did not seem able to get any spiritual help to her at all. So the next day before going to see her I asked Brother Renbeck whether people have to be saved before they can be healed. He said that he did not know. I then mentioned the fact of the ten lepers being healed and that only one returned to give glory to God; and, moreover, that I believe if we would pray for her the Lord would heal her and that God would get glory out of it some way. "All right," he said, "you talk to her today."

We went in to her room and I said to her "Martha, do you believe that God will heal you if we pray for you?" "Yes, the Lord healed Miss B. all right." I then said, "Are you willing to throw out all your medicine bottles and never go back to them again, even if the pain should return?" She called her father in and asked him to take the medicine bottles and smash them up. He went out and brought in a bushel basket and gathering them up, took them out and smashed them into pieces. Then we anointed her and prayed and while we were still praying she stretched out her hands and her feet. When we removed our hands she wrapped the sheet around her, jumped out of bed and ran around the house.

About six or eight months later while I was holding a meeting in Grand Forks, one evening a young lady of about nineteen years of age came into the service carrying her younger sister, nine years of age, who could not walk. I went right to them and asked where they were from and why they had come. The young lady told me they were from Grafton. She said, "I have not been well for a year, and about two years ago my sister, with some other children, was playing on the roof of an old shed and she either jumped or fell down, her heel struck a stone and her limb became withered. We have been to many specialists and none of them could help her. We heard that the two healers that healed Martha Gaulbright were here and we have come to be healed." I told her those men were no healers; that it was the Lord who healed Martha. "Well," she said, "the ministers, then." I asked her if Miss Gaulbright was still well? She answered, "She has never been sick since."

I told the young lady that only one of the ministers

was here. The next day Brother Emil Krutz came and we prayed for a large number of the sick, (39 in all), however, before we got through praying the two girls were gone. On inquiring whether anyone knew where they had gone, I was told they had either gone to the Hotel or to the Great Northern Railway station. I rushed to the station two blocks away as I was anxious to find out whether they had been healed, but I knew neither their names nor their address. When I got to the station I inquired about the train to Grafton to find the train was just pulling out.

The next summer on coming to the North Dakota State Camp meeting at Grand Forks, I was two days late having come from the South Dakota camp meeting, a little girl came running toward me as I was coming on the grounds, saying, "Praise the Lord, Brother Susag." I said, "Amen, who are you?" She said, "Don't you know me?" I said, "No, I see so many little girls and they all look alike to me." She said, "I'm the little girl who came to Grand Forks last winter and could not walk." I set my grip down and wept for joy, and said, "Please tell me, sister, when you commenced to walk." She replied, "My sister carried me to the train in Grand Forks; when we got to Grafton my short, dried up leg was just as long and as natural as the other one, so I walked home. Now mother is here at the meeting to get saved."

———: : : : ———

At one of the camp meetings at St. Paul Park as I was coming back from the baptismal service that we had in the river, I saw a young lady across the street walking with crutches, one limb seemingly, just hanging helpless. I felt sorry for her and went across the street and spoke to her. I asked her if she had been hurt or had had an accident.

She did not answer me at all. I said, "Do not be afraid of me. I am a minister; I am sorry for you and am anxious to know what your trouble is." Then she said, "I have tuberculosis of the leg, there are seven holes in it. I am just out of the Sanitarium at Saint Paul. They tell me that they can do nothing for me." I said, "Too bad, I am sorry for you." Then I asked her if she were a Christian; she broke down and wept. "Indeed, too bad," I said, "A young lady in that condition and yet not a Christian." Then I said, looking toward the camp grounds, "Do you see that tent over there? We are holding services in it and if you will come to the service tonight and get saved, God will heal you." She then left me and I went over to the tent.

She came to the service that night and when the altar call was given she went forward to seek salvation. When the altar service was over she was still there on her knees. Brother C. H. Tubbs had been instructing her and he said to her, "You can go and sit down now." But she pointed at me and said, "That man said that if I got saved that I could get healed too." Brother Tubbs said "alright" and went over to her with his oil vial and let a drop fall on her forehead. She dropped her crutches and ran down the aisles before we could pray, but the strength of her limb did not seem to hold out. So she came back to the altar and prayer was offered, but she was unable to use her limb.

Her mother was there. They lived in St. Paul and as it was some little distance to the station and the time was drawing near for the departure of the train, the mother said to her, "Take your crutches and let us go." But she answered, "Mother, I'll never touch those crutches anymore." "But if you can not walk, what are you going to do?"

Two young ladies helped her to the station and her mother carried the crutches. Two months after the camp meeting I went to Saint Paul Park and I met this same young lady, Sister Davis, as she came walking along as spry as any young lady. I said to her, "When did you get your healing and start walking?" She answered, "When we got to Saint Paul I got up and walked home and was well!"

——— : : : : ———

Brother Emil Krutz and I were called to pray for Grandma Dahl who was ill with double pneumonia. There were eight saints in the room and I heard one ask another, "How old is Grandma?" The reply was, "Seventy-seven years old," to which someone answered, "If I were that old I would not care to get well."

We anointed and prayed for the sick woman but she showed no signs of life or of getting any help. Brother Krutz looked at me and said, "The Lord heard prayer." We went into another room and closed the door, Brother Krutz said to me, "You go in there and send the folks out." We went back into the room and asked visitors to kindly step out of the room; then locking the door we again offered prayer. When we took our hands off this time the sister sat up in bed and said, "Call my daughter, Mrs. Umden, and tell her to bring me something to eat, I am so hungry." She was perfectly well and lived several years longer.

——— : : : : ———

For a year or more I was having pain in my liver. I was prayed for a number of times but did not even get relief and my body kept swelling up until I could hardly wear my clothes. The Ministry advised me to go to a specialist and find out what the trouble was and said then if I were healed God would get more glory out of it, so I went to the specialist.

The doctor said that it was not cancer, but worse still, it was enlargement of the spleen. He then said, "Dear man, there is no remedy for your trouble; I can only make a harness that you can wear suspended from your shoulders to help support your stomach, which will be some relief."

When I got home I told wife what the doctor had said and that I had made my last trip in the ministry. She looked at me and said, "No, you are not going to die." "Well," I replied, "I have been in this world fifty-six years and that is a long time, so if the Lord sees fit to take me I will be satisfied." She went out of the room and when she returned I saw she was crying and lifting her right hand she said, "You are not going to die." "How do you know," I asked? "The saints will not give you up," she answered.

A short while after this I was thinking that I would like to go to Arlington, South Dakota, now called Badger, before I died. I had raised up that congregation and they were very kind and dear to me. So I dropped Brother Gesselbeck a card asking him to meet me at Estaline on a certain date. Estaline was thirteen miles from Brother Gesselbeck's home. I arrived at Estaline about 6 A. M., but there was no Brother Gesselbeck there! I walked to a restaurant across the street and asked if any one knew Brother Gesselbeck. Yes, they knew him and why was I inquiring? I then told them my plight, that I was expecting him to be there to meet me. "Well," the man said, "Mr. Gesselbeck is an honest man and if he had gotten your card he would have been here, but yesterday was Washington's birthday, a holiday, and he will not get your card until after five o'clock this evening!

Well, here I was in a bad predicament—no money to go back home, no telephone out there and so ill that I could not walk over a block or two at one time. I was wearing my heavy winter clothes beside a heavy dog-skin fur coat. I left my grip at the restaurant and, walking across the street, found a long pole and started out on a thirteen mile hike. I would walk a little and then sit down, and even lie down a while and rest in the snow, and wept and prayed.

It was about five-thirty in the afternoon when I reached Brother Geselbeck's pasture. It had taken me over eleven hour to walk the thirteen miles. I was praying and weeping when I saw Brother Geselbeck coming from his mail box with my card. He looked up and saw me, then lifting his hand with the card in it, shook his head as if to say, "Poor Brother Susag!" In order to prove to him that I was not dead yet, I threw away my pole and jumped as high as I could and when I came down I was perfectly healed and the swelling was all gone! I had thought that this would be my last trip to Brother Geselbeck's, but I have made many since then.

———— : : : : ————

Once I was holding a meeting in North Dakota about ten miles in the country north of Denbeg. The morning after the meeting closed, I woke up and lay awake a while, then fell asleep again and I had a dream. I dreamed that I saw Brother and Sister Gaulke driving on the highway south of Grand Forks. Suddenly I saw the car go up in the air amidst a cloud of dust. Some folks came and took Sister Gaulke out of the wreck and laid her on a blanket, then a big black blanket came up between me and Brother Gaulke and the wreck. When I awakened it was just fifteen minutes past seven. It made such a vivid impression on me that I said to the family with whom I was staying, "I will not leave here until the mail carrier comes; I expect a telegram." I then told them my dream. They went with me to the mail box a mile from the farm, and when the mail carrier came, he had brought me a message from Mrs. Johnston telling what had happened at exactly the hour I was having my dream, and asking me to come at once, so instead of going to my next appointment I went at once to Grand Forks. On my arrival at the hospital when Sister Gaulke saw me, she said, "Of all the angels in heaven, how did you get here?" Sister Gaulke recovered but her husband lingered a few days and then went home to glory.

———— : : : : ————

I had a dream one time while I was in Europe about my second son who was working in a store in Superior, Wisconsin. I saw him go to a music store and buy a special instrument. I woke up and couldn't go back to sleep again, so got up and wrote to him, telling him that it was all right that he bought the instrument, for I knew he was interested in music, but I asked him to please not join an ungodly band as it might lead him into temptation and into bad things which would "bring down his daddy's gray hairs with sorrow to the grave."

He wrote back and thanked me for my letter but never mentioned a word about the instrument. A few days later I came home from Europe and he had resigned his position and gotten another one. His grips and trunk were brought to the house. The family were anxious to see what he had in them for he had been gone several years, so when they finally got to the big trunk he lifted his hand and looking at his mother and the rest, said hesitatingly, "I don't know, now . . . " His mother said, "Clarence, have you got something in your trunk you do not want us to see?" He answered, "Daddy knows." I said to him, "It is all right, Clarence; I am sure you obeyed my admonition." He opened the trunk and there was a new violin! Then he told us that when he was buying the violin he had intended to join an orchestra, but when he got home from the store with his violin there was daddy's letter. This fulfilled the Scripture that "Before they call I will answer and while they are yet speaking I will hear."

———: : : : ———

Another time before I went to Europe there was a little difference or misunderstanding between two ministers, and some other ministers were called on to help get the misunderstanding out of the way, which we did, and everything was fine. They were good ministers and I loved them dearly. They had both been a blessing to me. A year later I dreamed that the brother mostly to blame got up early one morning and traveled three hundred miles by train to see the other brother, and on seeing him treated him very unmercifully. I dreamed this at two o'clock in the morning and could not sleep any more, so got up and wrote this brother a kind letter telling him of my dream and that the Lord had shown me that he was now greatly to blame. I advised him that if the dream did not fit to destroy the letter and to resist the enemy, and also that I was praying for him. On coming back to America I learned that the dream did fit exactly as to the time, both date and hour, in which his unmerciful action took place.

———: : : : ———

While at the Anderson Camp Meeting one year, I dreamed that I saw the ministers of the Church of God within a large enclosure, walls four square, high and very beautiful. I was standing just inside the door, and on the outside of the door stood one of the leading ministers among us. He had gotten into some false doctrine, and he and his wife had built a little shanty just outside the walls near the entrance, where they had twelve to twenty ministers with them. The room was so small that they all had to stand up.

The brother was talking to me trying his best to get me to join his group and accept his doctrine. Then as I looked up the street, to my left as it were, I saw a troop of cavalrymen mounted on white horses and dressed in white uniforms, coming toward me. The troop was so long it seemed almost as though there was no end to it. An officer, who was riding on the side, said to me, "You stay in there with the rest of them and you will be protected." Then they went to the shanty, a little hut made of unpainted lumber, and smashed it up, scattering all the men inside. Then the clock struck two.

At the minister's meeting in the morning I asked if I might tell my dream and, consent being granted, I told my dream. After I had told it, Bro. E. E. Byrum got up and said, "I can interpret the brother's dream: We were dealing with this brother and sister until two o'clock this morning, and we found it to be an ungodly spirit and doctrine. I warn everyone to stay away from it." The couple left us and never came back again.

Brother George W. Green and I once came from Pit, a little town in northern Minnesota. On our way to Grand Forks we stopped at a town by the name of Steiner, the home of the Koglin family. Quite a number of people were in the house when we arrived. Grandma had had several strokes and the family had been looking for my address, as they were expecting she would die and wanted me to come and conduct her funeral services. We asked if we might see her and they told us we could. We went into the bedroom and prayed for her and the Lord healed her. If I remember correctly, she lived for over ten years longer.

———— : : : : ————

At one time I was holding a meeting in a school house near Warren, Minnesota. I was staying with a family named Keutzer, three miles from the school house. In the afternoon previous to the evening service I was praying, and wrestling with the devil. I asked the brother to start at least an hour ahead of time to go to the meeting or else give me a lantern and I would walk over. He asked me why, and I told him that the devil was mad at me and will not let me ride—that when I get in the car, it will stop.

The brother laughed at me and said, "I have a new Oldsmobile car," and they would not let me have a lantern, but when they were ready to go I got the lantern and told them to go on and tell the folks that I would be coming as fast as I could. But the brother said, "Get in the car." I didn't want to, but he took hold of me and almost forced me into the car. I got in and it ran for a rod or two and then stopped. I jumped out of the car, took the lantern and ran. After a while they caught up with me and stopped for me to get in, saying that if I didn't, they would not go. This happened several times. I would get in the car, it would run a rod or two and stop. Finally I ran away from them and walked all the way to the school house and they arrived after I got there. We were so late the people were just getting ready to leave, as it was nearly nine o'clock.

We all went into the school house and went on with the service. We found afterwards why the devil opposed me and did not want me there. There was a bootlegger in the audience, who, when hearing me relate the experience, got to thinking about it, became convicted and got saved. When we were leaving to go home, Brother Keutzer asked me how I was going to get home; was I going to walk? "No," I said, "I am going to ride and we will have no trouble with the car." The devil had lost his hold on that bootlegger and we had no further trouble with the car.

———— : : : : ————

The first time I was called to the Koglin home to hold services was in winter and very cold. The address given me was Thief River Falls, but did not state the number of the rural route, so there was no way for me to get to their place that evening, and I had only enough money to take me to Steiner, which was my destination. I asked at the depot whether I could stay there, but they said "No," because they closed up over night. So I left my grips there and went out to see what I could find, for there was no one in the city that I knew. I saw a light in a chapel and went in, thinking I might get an opportunity to testify, and that someone might invite me home with them. I got a chance to testify all right, but no one invited me to go home with them. I walked around the city and went into a restaurant, sat down and got warmed up. But soon they closed.

I kept walking the streets to keep warm, and after a while a man caught up with me and said, "Well, some one else is out walking in this cold weather, twenty below." I agreed that it was surely cold. He asked me whether I lived there, and I told him that my home was in Paynesville,

Minnesota. Then he said, "What is your name?" I told him, "S. O. Susag," and he then replied, "I used to know a man by that name who was in the grocery business on Franklin and Minnehaha in Minneapolis." He turned to me in the darkness and said, "I am Erickson of the firm of Rudda and Erickson that used to be on Cedar Avenue in Minneapolis."

It turned out that he was a good friend of years ago, so he soon found out why I was there. He asked me whether I had a hotel room yet. I told him, no, that I was just looking around. Nevertheless, he offered me money to pay for a room at the hotel. I refused it, but he insisted, saying, "If our spare room was empty I would have taken you to my home, but we have friends from North Dakota visiting us today, but you come to our home for breakfast in the morning before you take the train." He never knew what a blessing he was to me in the hour of my great need.

———— : : : : ————

SPEAKING IN TONGUES

At the State Camp meeting at Wilmar, Minnesota, I was asked to preach in Scandinavian as there were some sixty elderly Scandivanian people who did not understand the English language. I agreed to do so. As soon as I had begun to preach the whole camp came in to listen. When the service was over people asked why Brother Susag did not preach in Scandinavian in the afternoon. Brother Ring told them that he had done so. However, they insisted that I had spoken in English, since the whole camp, they said, had come in and heard me preach in English. The fact is: I had spoken in Scandinavian and the Lord interpreted it to them in English.

THE FUR COAT

At one time I was in great need of a fur coat, for the winters are very cold in the northern states and Canada. So I set my heart on having a fur-lined coat listed in the Sears Roebuck catalogue for $57.25. I asked the Lord if I could have it and He answered, "Yes."

Shortly after this matter had been decided, a brother came to me and said, "You need a fur coat and here are ten dollars to start toward it." Others wrote sending money specifying that it was for a fur coat until I had $36.50. Then a whole year passed and nothing came. The following November I went to Rice Lake, Wisconsin to hold a meeting for Bro. E. G. Ahrendt. It was very cold and there was lots of snow. On my arrival Brother Ahrendt said to me, "Haven't you got a fur coat, Brother Susag?" I answered, "Yes." He said, "Why don't you wear it this cold weather?" I answered, "I have it by faith—have had it for a year and a half and have $36.50 laid by for it that was given me towards buying a coat, but the price is $57.25." Then Bro. Ahrendt went upstairs and was gone for a long time. When he came down again, he said, "Brother Susag, before you leave here you are going to have a fur coat." I said, "Is that faith or presumption?" To which he replied, "If it isn't faith, I have never had faith." I said, "Praise the Lord; good for you and good for me."

When the meeting was over Brother Ahrendt said, "Did you get the fur coat?" I told him, "No." He then asked me where I was going tomorrow night from here, and I told him that I was going ten miles out in the country to a little meeting house for a service. He said, "I'll go with you."

After the service that night Brother Ahrendt again

asked, "Did you get your fur coat?" I said, "No." Upon which he inquired where I was going that evening. I told him that a family had invited me to their home and had offered to take me to another railroad over which I would be able to reach home sooner. Brother Ahrendt declared that he was going with me until he saw my last foot safe in the train, "and," he said, "if you haven't got the fur coat by then I'll not know what to think of myself or my faith." (By way of explanation would say here, that the offerings I received went for my general expenses; the money for my fur coat was to come from other sources. The Lord had promised me the fur coat.)

That night I had a dream. I woke up about three o'clock in the morning, and as I stirred a little, Brother Ahrendt whispered, "Are you awake?" I told him I was. "Did you have a dream?" he asked. I answered, "Yes, a woman came to me and gave me four bills!" "The fur coat! the fur coat!" he excitedly said. We got so happy that we couldn't sleep any more and we shouted, "Glory to God!" We made so much noise that we disturbed the folks down stairs, and when we went down they said, "What is the matter with you brethren making so much noise?" We told them we were so happy that we could not help ourselves.

After a while the sister asked me to come out into the kitchen. She gave me a chair and I sat down. She at once began to unburden her mind and said, "Did you understand when I spoke to you at the campmeeting at St. Paul Park three or four years ago that I was intending to give you some money for your trip to Europe?" I answered, "Yes, I thought so." "But" she said, "you said you had the fare." "Yes," I answered, "I had it by faith." Then in surprise, she asked, "But didn't you have the money in your possession? Weren't you then already on your way to Europe?"

"I was on my way to Europe," I answered, "but did not have all my fare—only by faith."

She then told me that she had been sick for about two years. She said, "I have been prayed for often, and have received some help, yet I gradually got worse. Finally," she said, "I got desperate about it and said to the Lord, 'What's the matter with me anyway; I cannot get well and I cannot die?' Then the Lord said, 'Do you know the Brother you intended to give some money before he went to Europe?' I said, 'Yes, in a way but he's back now.' The Lord said, 'That does not make any difference; how much was it?' 'Fifteen dollars,' was my answer. 'That's right,' the Lord said, 'but there is ten dollars interest on that now.' 'I'll give it to him the first time I see him,' I said. Then I was prayed for and healed at once." Having said this, she handed me the money, "Here it is," and it was FOUR BILLS! I took it and commenced to shout the glory of God. In came Bro. Ahrendt and I held up the four bills for him to see. He shouted, "The fur coat, the fur coat!" Then I related my experience to her of my praying for a fur coat and said to her, "If you had given me the money when I came back from Europe I would not have had to suffer cold for about a winter and a half." The sister was healed and blessed, and I was kept warm for many a day inside that fur coat.

——— : : : : ———

A number of years ago I was called to go to Wales, North Dakota, to hold a meeting at Brother Paul Garber's home, which was a Great Northern box car. The weather was very cold, the temperature being twenty degrees below zero. After the first evening service a woman came to me and said, "I am the sheriff's wife and I want you to come home with me. I cannot allow you to stay here." I went with her and the next day we got the Methodist church in which to hold our services.

More than half the people who attended the services were Catholics. On the last evening as I was going out of the church, the butcher of the town shook hands with me, putting three silver dollars in my hand and said, "You come back soon."

I surely had a fine stay with the sheriff and his wife, and the day I was leaving the sheriff was at the depot with a delegation representing the business men of the town saying to me, "We wish you would come back soon." I said to them, "What's your reason for wanting me to come back soon, since the butcher was the only business man of the city who came out to my meeting?" "When you come back," they said, "we will all come to your services, because many people have come and paid up their old bills and made good their outlawed notes since you have been here." I am sorry that I never had the opportunity of going back there again.

A number of the saints at Wales moved to Grand Forks, N. Dakota, and were a great blessing and an asset to that congregation. Later on, sixty-three adults and children moved to Benton Harbor, Michigan, and I understand that an English and a German congregation was started at that place through their efforts.

———— : : : : ————

One time Brother Renbeck and I went to Bro. Bahr's to pray for Willie, a son of theirs, who had the scarlet fever, and after we had prayed I felt that I should stay a little longer. I lay down on the lounge and fell asleep. All of a sudden Sister Bahr called and said, "I believe

Willie is dying," and when I laid my hands on him he was so hot that the heat seemed to go right through my whole body. I kept on rebuking the sickness and the devil, but it didn't seem to help any.

I prayed, "Lord, heal this boy to Thy glory. If no other way, I am willing to take this sickness upon myself, just so you get the glory of healing the boy." In a few minutes he was sound asleep, perfectly healed! But I felt as though I was sore all over my body. When I went out into the cold winter weather the cold would smart what seemed to be sores on my face, and when I got to the chapel to preach I felt ashamed to get up before the audience because I thought the folks would see the sores on my face, although I knew it was an imposition of the devil. When I got into the pulpit I told the people how I felt, and asked them to pray, and immediately the feeling left me. I learned the lesson NOT TO BE WILLING TO TAKE A DEVIL'S SICKNESS in order to get people healed.

——— : : : : ———

In 1942 as I was coming from the West coast to Wolf Point, Montana, I took the bus thirty-eight miles from there where another road turns off to go to my son's place, a mile and a half off the highway. It had snowed quite a bit and was somewhat stormy, but I thought I could make it. However, I had not walked far until I had to throw my grips into the ditch and tried to go on, but the snow was so deep I could not make it walking. My only way was to lie down in the road and ROLL. I kept that up quite a while, and when I got tired I would just lie and rest. After I had gotten a quarter of a mile I was so worn out that it seemed as though there was no hope for me. I rolled over to a fence post and stood up and tied myself to it, thinking that if I did freeze to death folks would be able to find my body. After I had been standing quite a while praying, I felt as though I was getting my strength again, so I loosened myself from the fence post and started to roll again and then tried to walk on my knees, but that would not do. The snow was too loose—I went down. Toward evening I had reached the highest spot from which I could be seen from my son's house. He was coming from the barn and happened to see me, and then quickly came to meet me and very soon led me safely to his home. So the Lord had mercy on me once more.

———— : : : : ————

One time I received a telegram from Brother Fortner of Brookings, S. Dakota asking me to come at once. I arrived there late in the evening and found that their son, Clarence, was seriously ill at the hospital in Huron, eighty-three miles from Brookings. The folks thought we had better wait until the following morning to go. Brother and Sister Fortner, another son, and the pastor all went with me in my car.

Clarence had been saved but had gotten away from the Lord. On our trip from Brookings, on the highway we drove eighty miles an hour and the pastor said, "Brother Susag, you do not need to go so fast." I thought that I would slacken down but the car was still going eighty miles; the pastor called again, "Brother Susag, you need not go so fast." I said nothing but felt rather sad that I was hurting the pastor's feelings, but still I was going EIGHTY. Finally the pastor spoke sternly, "Brother Susag, you don't need to go that fast." I felt sad, but said nothing, yet in spite of myself and the pastor, I was still going eighty miles an hour.

On arriving at the hospital the young man said, "I have gotten back to the Lord and this morning at three o'clock He said to me that at nine o'clock Brother Susag would be here to take you home." He had the clock standing on the chair and it was just nine o'clock when we arrived! The pastor walked out. (This occurred before the laws governing speed went into effect, but law or no law, the Lord wanted me there at nine o'clock.)

GETTING IN TROUBLE FOR OBEYING THE WORD OF GOD

A brother minister got the idea in his mind that wife and I were covetous, but we did not at the time realize to what extent it had affected him. Previous to his leaving the state he brought the matter before the body of ministers so as to have them deal with us. The ministers told him that they had not seen any indication of coveteousness in Brother and Sister Susag, and then asked him what proof he had for thinking so. He answered, "They do not give enough." (Our custom was never to tell anyone what we gave, because the Bible says, "Let not your left hand know what your right hand doeth.")

We were called before the Ministerial Assembly and the matter was taken up. The brethren said that they had not seen any indication of coveteousness in us and all the brother had against us was that we hadn't been giving enough, and, said they, "After thinking it over, neither did we know what you were giving." To which I replied, "If I'm coveteous, I'm the one that ought to know it, so won't you brethren, please help me out?" This is what they suggested: "You tell us how much you give and then we can compare." I answered, "If I tell you how much I give, won't it be fair for you folks to tell how much you give?" Whereupon the chairman replied, "Yes, that will be fair; I know you cannot give as much as me since my income is larger; but you and Bro. A— should give about the same amount." So they all told what they had given for the year. I then added the amounts and found the total, and getting my grip, took out of it receipts for what wife and I had given and asked the brethren to add them up. Then I requested them to add up what the seven ministers had given and, to the great surprise of all of us, they found that wife and I had given $22.50 more than all seven ministers together. This was one of the "ALL THINGS" in my life.

———: : : :———

When I was the evangelist at a certain State Camp meeting, a lady, who had only been to our services that morning, got saved at that Sunday morning service, and having to leave the meeting right away, wanted to be baptized before going. Three sisters came to me in protest, and said, "You are not going to baptize that woman with all those rings on, are you?" I answered, "Please leave that sister and her rings alone." To which they replied, "If you baptize that woman with all those rings, we will never have confidence in you again." I answered, "I'm very sorry, but let's pray about it; you go over in the timber in that direction and I will go over in this direction in the timber and pray and prepare for the baptizing."

As the woman, who was to be baptized, stepped into the water, she exclaimed, "Oh!" as if something was hurting her, then stripping the rings off her fingers she threw them into the sand, never more to put them back on her fingers.

In response to an urgent call to come to St. Paul Park I forthwith prepared to go, although not knowing the reason I was summoned. When ready to start, at the request of my wife, I consented to take along a rag carpet which she had made for the Old People's Home out there. I put the carpet into a sack and checked it to St. Paul, rechecking it from there to St. Paul Park. The baggage man asked me whether I had a trunk or a grip. I informed him I had a sack. In answer to his inquiry as to what was in it, I told him, "Clothing." While riding on the next train the devil said to me, "You're a pretty nice preacher; you lied to the baggage man; instead of telling him clothing was in the sack you should have said it was cloth or rag carpet." "Well," I said, "I can make that right on my return trip."

On my arrival at the Park I found that Brother Krutz had lost his mind. When I met him he did not know me. I went to praying and tried to talk to him and after a while he knew me. He said, "Brother Susag, Brother Susag, you are pure gold, pure gold." Then looking at me intently, pointing his finger at my heart, he said, "What do I see, a tiny spot?" No doubt the enemy wanted to hinder me in praying for him. The incident bothered me a little bit, so I went out into the woods and the Lord showed me that it was just an imposition of the devil to bother me. Brother Krutz was prayed for and the Lord healed him and the next Sunday he preached.

——— : : : : ———

PRAYING FOR EGGS AND KEROSENE

Brother Ahrendt and I were holding some meetings in the locality between Bertha and Hewitt, Minnesota. We were staying in a log house—just the two of us. We ran out of kerosene, and were also out of money. Brother A—

took the can and started to walk to Hewitt—a distance of six or seven miles—in the snow, hoping to meet some brethren who would ask him why he was carrying that can—but he met no one. He went to the post office, got the mail and concluded that he would have to go back without the kerosene; however, on opening one of the letters a dime dropped out. He immediately went to the store, bought the kerosene and returned home.

One evening Brother Ahrendt said to me, "Brother Susag, I'm hungry for some eggs; let's pray the Lord to send us some eggs." I replied, "How can we expect to get eggs out here? I haven't seen any chickens around here, nor in the bush where I have been." "Well," he said, "the Lord can bring them from somewhere." That evening on our returning from service we found something setting on the table covered with a newspaper. Brother Ahrendt lifted the paper and found a tiny basket with five eggs in it! I said, "You get three of them; you prayed and had faith while I only said, amen."

———— : : : : ————

THE READING ON THE SIGN POST CHANGED(?)

One day Bro. Ahrendt was out advertising the meeting. His last call was at a schoolhouse, and from there he wanted to go to Bertha intending to take a short cut through the brush to the highway. On coming to the highway, he saw a signpost pointing in the direction he was going, which read, "One mile to Hewitt." "Well," he thought, "what won't boys do changing the road signs?" He walked on a few steps and saw a little town not far away, then he realized that he had been going north while he thought he was going south. The boys had not done any harm. He was mistaken in his sense of direction.

One year Brother H. A. Sherwood was the evangelist at the Minnesota State Camp meeting which was held at Saint Cloud. A large, roomy church building was used for the services. The heat was record-breaking that year, and on one of the hottest afternoons when Brother Sherwood was expecting to preach as usual, the heat was so intense that he was physically unequal to the occasion, and so it came about that at Brother Sherwood's urgent request, Brother Allison F. Barnard (who, with Mrs. Barnard, was attending the meeting) consented to preach in his stead that afternoon.

As Bro. Barnard came into the pulpit the Holy Spirit came upon him and upon the whole congregation in such a way and in such measure as I had never seen in any service. The heat in the chapel moderated at once, but outside it was as hot as ever. It was as though the dear man was "out of the body" and there was no trouble at the altar of prayer for seeking souls to receive their heart's desire. They PRAYED THROUGH! So, again, the Scripture was fulfilled, "Not by might, nor by power, but by my Spirit, saith the Lord of hosts."

———: : : :———

Speaking of Brother Sherwood, I loved that big little man in the Lord. On one occasion he was the campmeeting evangelist at Morden, Manitoba, Canada. The Lord used him mightily and when the meeting was over it was arranged that wife and I should take him with us in our car to Grand Forks, North Dakota. It started to rain and did really pour down. The first forty-five miles the roads were nothing but black gumbo, and we used eight gallons of gas driving that forty-five miles.

Brother Sherwood sat in the back seat, praying all the time that we would not get stuck in the mud nor slide down into the ditch, and when we reached the gravel road in North Dakota he said, "Brother Susag, will you stop awhile so we can have a thanksgiving meeting right here, that the Lord has heard prayer and protected our lives!" And that is what we did. Brother Sherwood then said, "Bro. Susag, will you accept an admonition from a younger man than yourself?" I answered, "Any time, Brother." And he said, "This is the second worst automobile ride I ever had in all my life. Will you promise me never again to start out driving when the road is as bad as this?" My reply was: "Hello! Hello! Hello! Who is this? Brother Sherwood? What do you want? Your wife sick? What, dying? Yes, I'm starting out right away; I'm coming as fast as I can." Whereupon Brother Sherwood reached out his hand and said, "Brother Susag, forgive me; how quick a man can be to ask a promise of a man without thinking!"

———: : : :———

Once I was called to attend a meeting north of St. Cloud, Minnesota. There were about thirteen ministers there. It was among a people who were called, "The Free." Some three of their leading brethren had heard the Truth, and they were the ones who had sent for me to come. The ministers and the majority of the people were opposed to our teachings. When the offering was divided among the ministry, those three brethren, who were on the board, gave me $38.00.

But after I had taken the money I could not keep it on my person. I tried my best, but even when in my overcoat pocket the money burned me, so I gave it back to the brethren. A brother was going to drive me to the nearest railroad station, and when I had taken my seat in the buggy ready to go to town, these three brethren came and gave me fifteen dollars, saying, "We have given much more in the offering than that," and they felt that the fifteen dollars would not burn me. So I took the money and thanked them for it and we went on our way to town. As I put the money in my pocket it still burned me. I had to take it out again and lay it on the bottom of the buggy. I told the driver to take it back and return it to the brethren. He said, "They will not know what to do with it now that the meeting is ended." I told him of a young minister who was sick and in need—to take the money to him. I was needing the money badly, even the $38.00, as I was without money to pay my way home.

As we crossed the railway track coming into the town near the depot, I asked the man to let me off. As I was walking up to the station a man, whom I did not know, came along beside me and pressed a five dollar bill into my hand, and that was enough to take me home! A number of people took their stand for the truth in that meeting.

———: : : :———

THE LORD STILL HEARS PRAYER

At a Ministers' Meeting at Tulare, California, in 1945, while the noon lunch was being served, I was sitting in the chapel with my head bowed on the chair in front of me, praying for a certain amount of money, not expecting any money at that meeting. Soon I felt the confidence that the Lord had heard prayer and dismissed the matter from my mind. A few minutes later a man came and sat down beside me and said, "Say, how do you get your expenses; do you get a salary for traveling around this way?" I answered, "No, I have no salary; I pay my expenses as the Lord puts it into the hearts of the brethren to give to me." "Well," he said, "the Lord told me to come over and give you this."

And he handed me the very amount I had been asking the Lord for!

———— : : : : ————

Brother Renbeck and I were holding a meeting out near Kellys, North Dakota. After the service one afternoon I saw Brother Renbeck sitting in a corner of the room weeping. I went over to him and asked him what was the trouble. He said, "I am weeping because there were not more sinners in the meeting to get saved, for if there had been more there, more would have been saved." To which I replied, "Keep on weeping."

———— : : : : ————

MY FIRST EXPERIENCE IN DEALING WITH DEVIL POSSESSION

Another time we were holding meetings near and in Fosston, Minnesota. It was said of us that "those preachers are of the devil." One evening a man came to the meeting who had blood poisoning in one of his knees. In getting to the meeting he used a long pole to help support himself. He wanted to see those preachers who were "of the devil." When he arrived the room was full and there being no chair for him to sit on, I gave him mine. When we knelt down to pray I laid my hands on his knee and asked the Lord to heal him and he was healed instantly.

A few nights later a man came to the service who was possessed with devils. He was frothing at the mouth and acting like a madman. As I took hold of him and laid my hands on him we almost wrestled. I commanded the devils to come out of him, and I told the Lord I would never let Him go until He delivered the man, and he was finally delivered by the Spirit of the Lord. Although it was winter time I was as wet as though I had been dipped in the river. While the struggle was going on all the people ran out of the room. But the man was fully delivered and then he was saved.

———— : : : : ————

In another of our meetings a sister got saved and received light on baptism. She had a little baby girl and her husband wanted to have the child sprinkled, as that was his faith. The mother was to carry the baby forward to receive this rite, but she objected and said, "No, I cannot do that; but if you care to, you may do so, for she is as much yours as she is mine." But the husband would not consent to do that. Well, she didn't know what to do and went to Brother and Sister Anton Nelson for advice. Brother Nelson said, "Let us ask the Lord about it." After they had prayed about it, Brother Nelson said to the sister, "You go and carry the baby and we will come along and pray for you and it will all come out all right."

At the Sunday service that the baby was to receive this rite, there were seven children in all being subjected to this ceremony. The minister came to this sister and said, "What is the name of the child?" The sister answered, "Anna Marie." Then the minister said, "Anna Marie, do you forsake the devil and all his works? Do you believe on the Lord Jesus Christ and will you upon this faith be baptized?" (The mother was supposed to answer, "Yes.") The sister answered nothing. So he read his ritual once more and again no response. So after asking the question the third time, he said, "Anna Marie, don't you answer?" At this, the father of the child called out from the audience, and stamping his feet, said, "Come on, wife, that's enough!"

You will remember reading at the beginning of this book I told of how my mother, when I was a child, used to say to me, "Child, O child! You are more trouble to me than all the other eight children put together!" And yet, after I had been away in America for twenty-four years when I went back home the very first day my mother had me sit facing her not more than about four feet away and I listened to her telling me stories about the most wonderful boy I had ever heard of. After about two hours of this pleasant entertainment I smiled and said to her, "I have recollections of a mother who used to weep over this same boy and say, "O child, what shall I do with you, you are more trouble to me than all the other eight children together." "O Ja," she said, "but you were the best boy anyhow." I am fairly good in arithmetic, but that is a problem I have not solved yet.

———— : : : : ————

PREACHING ON WORLDLINESS

While conducting a revival meeting at Grand Forks, North Dakota, I preached one afternoon on the subject of worldliness. An attorney and his wife from Langdon, North Dakota were staying in the city to attend the meeting. After hearing this sermon the wife would not attend the services any more. At the close of the Sunday afternoon service, two days later, the attorney came to me and said, "The Holy Spirit was in the meeting this afternoon, wasn't He?" I replied that He was, and he continued, "Every sinner present was saved and something happened to me that I never remember having experienced before. I cried like a child!"

I asked him why his wife had quit coming to the meeting. In reply he asked, "Has Sister Hansen told you anything about us and our home?" I said, "Yes, you once gave a minister twenty-two-hundred pieces of money, they were all pennies. You did a good thing. This is all Sister Hansen ever told me about you folks. I have heard nothing whatever about you."

He referred to the sermon on worldliness and said, "In your talk, you practically, set a price on everything we have in the home, such as curtains, carpets, furniture and the range; and you illustrated it this way: 'Supposing a person could buy a suitable range for $42.50 but seeing another, just the same kind only with nickel-plated trimmings, for $82.00 and he would choose the latter, wouldn't that be called the pride of the eye?' And that is just the kind of range we have! and my wife could not see it that way." She thought that Sister Hansen had told me and did not get that out of her mind and was finally lost, the husband said.

I was preaching under the leading of the Holy Spirit and in what I said I had no one in mind in using that illustration, but was simply trying to show that such money could be used to better purpose and that sometimes when folks yielded to the temptation to take the finer appearing article they might be going beyond their means.

———: : : :———

One Sunday morning when I was pastor in Grand Forks and had just gotten through preaching a man came rushing up to the pulpit and said in a rough voice, "Who told you all about me?" I put out my hand and said, "My name is Susag, what is your name?" He answered, "You stood before this audience this morning and told them everything I have ever done!" I answered, "Dear man, I don't know you, nor have I ever heard of you, what is your name?" He looked around, then turned and out he ran! I never saw the man again.

Some years ago when in Norway, Morris Johnson and I held a meeting on a large farm in Roleg in Numedahl. A large crowd was out at the first service. We knelt down to pray and while we were praying I heard a great commotion and when we rose from our knees we found that two thirds of the people were gone. The foreman of the King's highway was in the audience and he had said when he came out there, that those preachers were too fanatical and if he had had his gun along and had shot them, he would have done the Lord a good favor. However, I do not think that in his heart he meant as bad as it sounded, for some time later he invited us to his home and treated us with much courtesy and kindness. A number were saved and baptized and quite a nice little congregation was raised up at that place.

———— : : : : ————

While we were at Sanes, Norway, Brother Morris Johnson was very sick and one evening when we arrived at our stopping place he rolled onto the bed with his clothes on, exhausted. He had been bleeding from the lungs and was so weak that I could hardly get him home. We wept and prayed and finally I said to him, "Morris, can't you get out of bed and kneel down with me and pray?" "I might," he said, "but I think the bed is the best place for me." However, he got down and said a few words and then rolled back into bed again. He wasn't able to undress all night and I was afraid to go to sleep for fear that he might leave me most any time during the night.

In the morning he seemed to be somewhat rested and I said to him, "Brother Morris, we must try and get down to Sister Svenson's and get you some meat broth." (Sister S. had a delicatessen store, and Morris hadn't eaten anything for a couple of days) but he said, "I am unable to get down there nor can I eat anything." "But," I said, "You've got to get down there even if I have to carry you there on my back. You'll have to eat or I will be having to bury you somewhere among the rocks in Norway." He got up and I put my arm around him and, as luck would have it the road was down hill. We had to stop and rest several times but we got there and the Lord must have impressed Sister Svenson for she had some broth all ready made, but as she was preparing to serve it the trouble in his lungs began again and he went to the wash room. I fell prostrate on the floor crying to God for help for him. Suddenly I realized I had received faith for him and called to him, "Morris, the bleeding stops, NOW!" And it did. And from that time on he recovered rapidly. (When I think of that dear brother and the plight he was in, it brings tears to my eyes, even now).

———: : : :———

A WONDERFUL MEETING AT STAVANGER

A telephone call came to Sr. Svenson from two ministers at Stavanger requesting the two American evangelists to come to them. We accepted the call and Sr. Svenson's daughter and Bro. Fjield went with us. How the ministers came to locate us at Sr. Svenson's I never knew, as neither of us had ever been at Stavanger. The names of the two ministers calling us were Johnson and Jornsen of the Christian church. We called first at Brother Johnson's where we were warmly welcomed. They told us that they had heard of us and had been earnestly praying for the Lord to send us to them and that they were glad we were there: "You are here in answer to prayer," they said, and then opening a door into another room informed us that there was our bedroom. They showed the dining room, saying, as they did so, "Anytime that you are hungry, come here and eat." To all this kind welcoming my response was, "This really seems to me to be like too much of an open door in face of the fact that you do not know us nor do we know you, perhaps we had better go in and have prayer together and some consultation about the matter. After we had had prayer they related the following:

"We belong to the Christian Church; formerly there were two hundred members of us or more, but two years ago a "Tongues speaker" an ex-Baptist minister, came to this city and as he seemed to be earnest and sincere we were sorry he was not getting a single opportunity to speak, so decided to give him the privilege to speak once in our chapel, and that was once too often! At the meeting, I (Bro. Johnson) was sitting on the platform with him, and Brother Jornsen, who weighed two hundred and sixty pounds, was standing in the aisle holding on to the back of a chair on which a man was sitting, as the chapel was packed. After the preacher had spoken ten or fifteen mintues seven women were lying on the floor in a trance.

"We took a stand against the spirit that was working and, talk about power! The chapel wall on one side cracked (the evidence of which was still to be seen)." Brother Jornsen said, "I took a stand against it with all my soul but nevertheless my feet went from under me and I was thrown to the floor and my jaws were just jabbering." "This continued eight days and nights until we finally got the victory over it and the preacher took over two hundred of the congregation with him, leaving us but nine persons, we two ministers make the total number eleven. And if you go with us to the service tonight there will be thirteen of us and we will have services, Sunday, Wednesday, Thursday and Friday, and" they added, "you must preach only until nine o'clock, the services start at eight fifteen. Don't let any women testify nor any pentecostals!

"Now," I said, "I will give you our proposition, we will go with you tonight and tomorrow you can advertize in the two city daily papers that two American evangelists are here to hold services every night including Saturday and three services on Sunday, all next week until Friday and then we will see how things go." "That will not do," they said, "No one will come out Saturday night nor Monday or Tuesday nights." "Well," I said, "you can let us have the key and if no one comes Brother Johnson and I can go inside and have prayer. Upon this condition we can stay, and if not, we will take our grips and go."

To which they replied, "You can't go, for the Lord has shown us that you are to hold a meeting for us." The next night there were about two hundred in the congregation and some ten minutes before nine o'clock eight persons started to get ready to leave; I was still speaking, so paused and said, "Just a minute, please: We have just come from Denmark where we preached as long as the Lord would lead, until nine or ten o'clock. Now if you have to go home you are welcome to go, but if it's simply your custom to leave a meeting at a certain time whether or not the service is over, we are going to pray the Lord to break up such a custom." Six of the persons sat down again and two left. Saturday night the chapel was full and Sunday night quite a number were saved. The meeting continued almost four weeks and souls were getting saved right along.

One day we had a baptizing service between two boat houses in the North sea and after I had baptized all the candidates, a fisherman, who owned one of the boat houses, came out and asked me whether I would not baptize him. On my inquiry as to his being saved, he told me this: "I was saved three years ago but have never before met folks with whom I believed the Lord was working, but today as I witnessed this service I was convinced that the Holy Ghost was with you folks. I baptized him and never saw him again. After that we were not allowed to baptize from the shore but had to take the folks out in a boat and baptize them from a rock in the North sea.

Following that incident we were invited to a sea Captain's home, to be there at 9:30, the next morning. The house was the most finely finished house I had even been in. When we arrived in the morning we found it was full of people of the upper class, the men with their silk hats and the women equally distinctive in their dress. Some of the company were saved and some fifteen more were saved that morning.

The lady of the house and her six sisters had a brother who was an old sea captain and was sick. We were told he was an infidel and would have nothing to do with preachers, that if any happened to come into his house he ordered them out. His seven sisters were praying earnestly for him and they felt that we could be a help to him. Their plan was to set a day when they would all go and visit him and if the weather was fine we were to come by and they would be on the porch talking to him. We were to pass along on the other side of the street and when they saw us they were to call "Good morning" and invite us over and introduce us to their brother, he was not to know that we were preachers. The plan was successful and after talking awhile Captain Parsons invited us into the house.

On coming into the room we noticed that the walls were hung with pictures of ships, thirty-eight steamers. He said he had been seaman on each one of them and captain on several. So he took us for a trip around the world.

Finally he came to the last one, a very large ship, but it looked like a rusty, broken-to-pieces tin can, its masts, smokestacks and bridges had evidently been blown or swept off. We were awed by the sight and said, "This looks bad." "Yes," he said, "that was the trying hour of my life, it was in a typhoon off the coast of Sidney, Australia. This is how it looked when we were towed in." Then I looked at my watch and found we had been talking for two hours and feeling that it was time for us to leave I said to him, "We are two ministers and generally when we make a call, before leaving we sing, read some Scripture and have prayer. Would you grant us that privilege here?" He said, "I see no reason why you should not do so."

We, accordingly, sang, read a Scripture lesson and had prayer, after which we said to our host, "We have certainly had a pleasant visit and enjoyed the trip around the world with you immensely, and now there is one sailing trip left for you to take. For all these other trips no doubt you made suitable preparation. What about this one; are you ready to meet your Maker in peace?" "No," he said, "The Lord doesn't have such bad men as me." But we told him that was just the kind He came to save. He said, "Boys, boys, you don't know what bad men seamen are." We tried to talk to him, but to no avail. So we thanked him and said Goodbye. As we left he said, "Boys, boys, come back soon."

The next day we heard that he was poorly and the Board of Health had ordered that no one shake hands with him as his case was not yet diagnosed. We continued to visit him, instructing him and praying with him. On one of these occasions on leaving him we both made a GOOD mistake. We broke down and wept. Morris speaking to me in English said, "I love this man's soul like my own father's and wouldn't lay a straw in the way of his getting saved;

I would like to shake his hand, but may not." "As far as I am concerned," I said, "I wouldn't be afraid to take his hand in both mine, but for the sake of the public we cannot do it; but he is a man of understanding, we will go and explain to him and I'm sure it will be all right." Later, as we were leaving, he said, "Be sure to come back soon."

The next day I was called out to an Island and Brother Morris went over alone to see him. He was up and apparently pretty well and he said to Morris, "Young man, you had better speak English. I understand your English better than I do your Norwegian." Now you can see that the mistake the day before was a good one. That day he got gloriously saved and the next day he was up and around happy and praising the Lord, at two o'clock in the afternoon he lay down to rest and went home to glory. On account of his salvation we were asked to speak to the students at the mission college.

Here at Stavanger a good congregation was raised up and Brother Mortensen became pastor, he was a tailor by trade and also was the owner of a fine clothing store. They got the chapel the revival was held in, in 1911, in 1922. I went through and they expected me to remain for a three weeks meeting to preach on Church of God doctrine. I was supposed to be there on Sunday, but did not arrive until Monday. They had advertised for three services for Sunday, and between fifteen hundred and two thousand were present for each service. I was unable to remain for the three weeks meeting as I was traveling through on a special mission for the Missionary Board and the boat left the next morning. Speaking of the truth, this would have been the greatest opportunity that Norway will have for years to come and perhaps ever.

Brother Mortensen said, "O how sad—this all happened

because of a crooked preacher that Brother Susag had to take back to America." Brother Mortensen raised up a number of congregations on the West coast, and in 1937 the old chapel at Stavanger was razed and a new and larger chapel was erected in its place.

———— : : : : ————

MY WIFE HEALED OF CANCER

Some years ago my wife had a sore on her left cheek. Dr. Morgan examined it and pronounced it cancer. She was prayed for and the third day after there was no sign of cancer.

A little later a growth started on her right side just above the hip. It grew until it was twenty-two inches long, sixteen inches by the body and fourteen inches around at the end of it. It finally developed into cancer. She was prayed for often but seemingly was not helped, the odor from it was horrible. We went to the Anderson Camp meeting. On the day especially set apart for the healing of the sick, and seats at that particular meeting were so arranged that for each sick person there were three preachers to pray for him or her. My wife came up and sat down on the chair next to the one where I was offering prayer, and after prayer had been offered for her, I heard one of the ministers say to her, "Sister Susag, do you believe the Lord heals you? She answered, "By faith I am healed." And the minister said, "Yes, by faith, is right." From that time the cancer began to fall to pieces.

On the way home I asked her what it was that gave her the faith for healing. She said, "I don't know; when I went onto the platform I wanted Brother and Sister Byrum to pray for me, and could have gotten on their chair, but there came a young lady who looked as though she might be in the last stages of tuberculosis, to such an extent was she affected that she had to be supported by a sister, one on each side of her when she attempted to walk, and I saw she was in greater need than I was, and, too, she was a young woman. I was willing for anyone to pray for me, and if I were healed or not it would be all right." I replied, "that is where you gained the victory."

This happened in the latter part of June and around the first of October there was nothing left but a red spot about the size of a dollar to show where the cancer had been. Just before we went to Anderson, a neighbor lady wanted to see the cancer and the sight of it made her so sick she was in bed for two days. And through it all my wife never once complained.

———: : : :———

On the last evening of a meeting I was holding in Whittier, California, a man came to me telling me of a sick lady who wanted me to come and pray for her. I consented to do so but told the man I must go quickly as a brother was coming very soon to take me to Los Angeles. On arriving at the bedside of the sick woman I asked her what her trouble was. She told me she had a cancer on her left breast and side, and that having to lie on the one side all the time she became very sick and sore. I prayed the prayer of faith for her and left immediately.

One year later I received a letter from her. She wrote, "It is just a year ago tonight since I sent for you to come and pray for me. As you prayed for me it was as though an electric shock went through me and after you left I turned over on my left side and went to sleep and slept all night and in the morning when I woke up I was perfectly healed. I have waited a year before writing, to see whether any symptoms returned, but none ever did."

In one of my meetings while I was pastor at Grand Forks I felt impressed to speak to a young man, Tom Perkins, a War No. 1 veteran. I went down into the audience to speak to him, and told him he ought to seek the Lord that night as something was going to happen. He said, "Do you think so?" I said, "No, I dont' think so, I KNOW so." But he said, "Not tonight." That was Sunday, and on Wednesday afternoon as I was going down DeMeres Avenue he came out of a clothing store with a friend of his, I said, "How do you do" to him and passed on in front of him, but as I was passing him the Lord said to me, "Go back and speak to Tom." I at once turned back to him and said, "Tom, listen to me; you ought to seek the Lord. Let us go back in the store and settle it with the Lord." But he said, "No." I said, "It is very important." He said as before, "Do you think so?" And again I answered, "I don't think so, I know so." He took it very nicely but refused to make any move toward seeking the Lord. Two days later, the following Friday, he went to Minneapolis and on Sunday afternoon he was crushed to death between two street cars. Would it not be well for people to heed the warnings of God's servants and His Spirit?

The pastor of the Scandinavian Free church at Brookings, South Dakota, one time sent for me to come to pray for a sister who was a member of his congregation and had been sick in bed for some six months. I preached there several times and then announced that I was going to pray for the sick sister at three o'clock the next day, and asked all those who had faith to be present and those who did not have faith to stay away, preachers and all. Only one person was there—an elderly Baptist sister from Huron—Sister Shall. The prayer of faith was offered and Sister Johnson was healed and was present at the service that evening.

One Sunday morning wife and I with two sisters drove to Westlake for the forenoon service which was held in the home of Brother and Sister Hans Myhre. After service wife came to me and said that Sister Myhre wanted us to stay for lunch. But I said, "No, we cannot stay for lunch, the Lord wants us to go home right away." On hearing this, Sister Myhre came to me and said, "You have got to stay for lunch." I answered, "Sister, we can't stay for the Lord told me to go home." She said, "And then the sisters will not get anything to eat either. Why do you have to go?" I said, "I don't know, only that the Lord says, go home." "Brother Susag, you are stubborn," the sister insisted.

We drove home. Wife went upstairs to change her dress, ready to get lunch. I sat on a chair meditating on what had taken place. I said to myself, "Are you stubborn? Why did you come home?" Just then the telephone rang. I answered and a voice said, "Is this Rev. Susag?" "Yes," I said. "Hold the line, long distance calling you," he informed me. After a short pause a voice said, "This is Anna Anderson of Brookings, S. D. Do you remember promising Grandma H., when you were pastor here, that you would officiate at her funeral? She died this morning and is to be buried on Tuesday. Can you come?" I told her I would come. As I turned from the telephone wife came into the room and I said to her, "Now I know why I had to come home so quickly, for if they had not gotten in touch with me now, I couldn't reach there in time for the funeral." She said, "Sometimes you are a little queer, but I have committed you to the Lord and things always come out all right."

———— : : : : ————

When Brother August Christofersen of Norway Lake, Minnesota, was down with double pneumonia I was sent for to come and pray for him. I went and prayed for him and the Lord raised him up. I stayed for three days, went home and in three or four days received a phone call to come back. I asked whether he was sick. They answered, "No, but he wants to see you." I was able to get a ride almost to his place, and walked the rest of the way. On nearing his home I turned in to a grove I had to pass and kneeled down to pray for the brother. The Lord said to me, "You do not need to pray for him now; he is home with me." On coming toward the house his brother came out to meet me, and I said to him, "So Brother August is home with the Lord!" He said, "How did you know?" I said, "The Lord told me over in the grove."

———— : : : : ————

While I was in Denmark I was invited to come to a certain town with which I was entirely unacquainted. Finally when I found time to go I went without writing to announce my coming. On arriving in the city I found I had forgotten both the name and address of my friends. I walked back and forth on the depot platform, racking my brain, as it were, to come across the needed address, but I just could not remember it. A man spoke to me and said, "You seem to be in deep meditation, or in trouble of some kind." I said, "I surely am." To which he replied, "Sometimes we get into such a fix; do you suppose I could be of any help to you?" But I answered, "I don't suppose you can." However, I told him my trouble. He laughed and said, "Surely you are in bad fix; can't you think of anything?" "The only thing I can think of," I said, "is that they are the parents of Mrs. Anna Nelson of Kaas, Denmark." "Well," he said, "you haven't struck it so bad after all—I am her father!"

When I was pastor in Grand Forks we had in the congregation a mother in Israel, a German sister who could not speak English. One Sunday evening the Lord had blessed in a spiritual way. Mother Calm said to Brother Shave, "I can preach Bro. Susag's sermon in German now." (I had preached in English.) Bro. Shave said, "You can't do it." But she said, "I can." At that, Brother Shave raised his voice and said, "Everybody wait a little while." And, sure enough, Sister Calm preached my sermon, the Germans said, "almost to a word."

———— : : : : ————

At the St. Paul Camp meeting one time, Sister Aamot came to me telling me she had lost a five dollar bill, over which she was feeling very badly. Her husband was not saved. She wanted me to pray that the Lord would help her find it. She told me she thought she had lost it on her way coming from the Old People's Home to the tabernacle. It had been blowing pretty hard that day and she had the bill in her handkerchief.

I went out into the timber to pray, and how the wind did blow! After I had been earnestly praying that the Lord would help me to find the bill for her and was getting up from my knees, on looking down into the leaves, lo, there, between my knees, was the five dollar bill! And the sister had no difficulty in proving that it was her five dollar bill.

———— : : : : ————

While still in Denmark, one time Brother Morris Johnson and I were holding a meeting on a farm. As we saw a large, fine looking man coming toward the meeting place, Morris said, "Let's go behind the barn and pray God Almighty to convict and save that man this afternoon." And the Lord honored our faith and really saved the man that afternoon.

———: : : :———

I was holding a meeting in Albert Lee, Minnesota and from there was intending to go to Greenwood, Wisconsin. I looked at my time-table to find out what the railroad fare would be and I figured it to be thirteen dollars, so asked the Lord to give me thirteen dollars that evening. At the close of the service someone put some money in my pocket and I began to thank the Lord for thirteen dollars. The devil said, "You haven't got thirteen dollars in your pocket," but I said I had. He said, "Just feel in your pocket and you will find there is hardly anything there, or take it out and count it and you will see." I told him that I would neither feel in my pocket nor count the money for him, and that I had thirteen dollars.

When I got to my room I knelt down and thanked the Lord for thirteen dollars, and then took the money out of my pocket and counted it and found I had $13.05. On buying my ticket the next day it cost $13.05! I had made a mistake in my figuring, but the Lord knew the exact fare.

———: : : :———

During the meeting at Greenwood I went out inviting folks to the services. One day I came to a farm house where the man of the house was ill in bed with tuberculosis of the spine. I told him that I was a minister and also, that I believed in Divine healing. When he heard this, he said, "You are the very man the Lord has sent to me that I may be healed." I said, "I do not know about that; however, I will pray for you. I am impressed of the Lord not to anoint you. I will be back on Friday afternoon, and in the meantime will pray the Lord to show me what to do." With this arrangement the sick man was satisfied. It was now dusk, and on reaching my room in the house where I stayed, I knelt down beside a chair to pray for him. As I did so, a cow and three sheep stood right before me. I did this four times, and as soon as I would get on my knees here were the cow and three sheep between me and God, so to speak. So I gave up trying for that time, but the next day at ten o'clock I went in to pray for him again in broad daylight. But as I did so, the cow and the sheep were there before me.

On the appointed Friday I went to see him again. He inquired at once what the Lord had made known to me about him. I told him the Lord had shown me something but that I did not understand what it meant. He was anxious to hear what it was, and I related the vision I had had. He said, "I perceive that the Lord has sent you to be a help to me," and continuing, went on to say, "We used to live in Iowa on a good sized farm and we were well-to-do financially. I was very much interested in spiritual work, even to printing and sending out a number of tracts. But it seemed that my poor soul was clinging to the worldly thing too much. I was troubled about it, off and on. However, your vision means that if I only had a cow and three sheep —which we have—if my soul is clinging to them I can never enter heaven." "Surely," he said, "the Lord has sent you to help me. Please pray that I get right with God; that is the main thing." The dear man bitterly repented and became very happy. The third day following this event he went home to glory.

———: : : :———

I had promised that after this meeting I would go to hold a meeting at Dallas, Wisc., but the Lord impressed me to go home. Knowing no reason for going home, I bought my ticket only to a certain station where I would have to change if I went to Dallas, thinking that maybe my feelings would change before I got there. But there was no change in my feelings when we got there, so I bought a ticket to St. Paul and from there got a ticket to Hawick, Minn., which is just three miles from my home.

On the street in Hawick, I met a young brother who exclaimed when he saw me, "Oh, so you got our postal card?" I replied, "I did not get any postal card." Then he said, "But you got the telegram?" I told him I had not received any telegram either. "Well, then," said he, "how did you happen to come home?" I told him that the Lord wanted me to come home, and then asked him what the trouble was. He told me that my wife was very sick, near to dying. Then he very kindly said he would take me out home. On arriving home wife said, "I knew you were coming; I asked the Lord to send you." She was suffering from an internal malady from which the nurse had told her she could not recover, and so made up her mind that she was going to die.

Right at this time we received a letter from Brothers Nelson and Niles requesting me to come and hold a tent meeting for them in San Antonio and that I should bring my tent with me to hold the meeting in. Of course, I felt I could not go and wrote them to that effect. Meanwhile, wife had persuaded me that she was going to die, and being in poor circumstances, I said to her, "You will not hold it against me, if when you die, I sell out and take a homestead and so get out of debt, will you?" And her reply was, "When I am dead you can do what you please."

Just about that time we got a letter from the Brothers Nelson and Niles telling us they had been praying and the Lord had showed them that Sister Susag was not going to die. On hearing this, wife said, "The good brethren do not know any better; I am going to die." (And I was thinking so, too, as she was getting no help.) More and more I was thinking about the homestead; but wife told me I had better go to Texas. It seemed almost impossible to get anyone to come and stay with her and the children, yet she would say, "We will get along some way and you had better go or else souls will be lost. If I should pass away before you get back you know where I am going and if you keep true to the Lord we will meet in glory."

But I did not feel as though I could go and leave her that way. A couple of nights after I had had this conversation with her I had a dream. I saw a little table standing beside my bed on which was a kerosene lamp. The light was just about to go out. It would light up a little and then go down till it looked as though it was just ready to quit burning. I saw Jesus standing on the other side of the table with a sad look on his face, pointing to the lamp and saying, "Your lamp is about to go out." And I awoke from my dream and jumped out of bed, ran into the next room and said to my wife, "On Tuesday morning, I leave for Texas whether you are living or dying." To which she replied, "Praise the Lord for your decision."

The Lord miraculously sent a good sister to our home from Washington. She arrived the morning I was leaving for Texas. When she discovered the circumstances, and that wife was sick, she said, "Now I know why the Lord sent me here, and I'm here to stay until Sister Susag is well."

So I went to San Antonio. This was in the year 1902. At one place where I had to change trains on the way, I took my grip and walked out on the platform toward the train I was to take. There I stood and did not get on the train, and the train pulled out without me. I walked back to the depot, and the agent asked me whether I had intended to take that train and why I did not get on it. I simply told him I didn't know why. "Well," he said, "you fool, you will now have to wait four hours and take a slow train." (I understood a little later why I was held back from boarding that train. Only forty-five miles out it became derailed and some forty passengers were seriously injured and, if my memory is correct, some were killed.)

When the tent meeting was over at San Antonio, Bro. Nelson left with me and we were expecting to stop over in Hamilton and Kingston, Mo. to hold some services. As we came closer to the first place Bro. Nelson said, "Here the saints are well-to-do people." So, I thought, if they are well-to-do we will not need to spend our time asking God for our car fare, for they well know that preachers need car fare. The congregation rented a room for us about a couple of blocks from the depot and we ate our meals in the different homes.

After the meeting had closed and we had gone to our room at eleven p. m., Brother Nelson asked me whether I had received money for our car fare. I told him I had not; that I thought he had received it all, since he had been there before. But he hadn't received any. We then decided we had better see whether we had enough money to take us to the next place. Brother Nelson had enough for his fare and eight cents over; I was lacking two dollars. We were to leave on the four-thirty train in the morning, and now we had to pray the Lord to get us the two dollars!

As for me, I was not acquainted in the city and did not know where to go to raise a penny. We prayed until two o'clock, then I said to Brother Nelson, "We do not need to pray any longer; the Lord says He will attend to it." We went to bed for about an hour and a half. We went to the depot and Brother Nelson bought his ticket, then I ordered mine and put what money I had in the window of the ticket office. While the agent was counting the money, a man came running very fast into the waiting room and stuck his left hand right in front of my nose through the ticket window and left two dollars there, then turned and went out so fast that I had no chance to thank him. Brother Nelson looked at the man, and then asked me whether I knew him, but I had never seen him before, nor had Brother Nelson. The lesson I learned from this incident was that it is better to depend upon the Lord than on well-to-do saints.

On arriving home I told wife of the incident. She at once asked me whether I was sure it was a man who brought the two dollars. I said, "To me he looked like an angel, and he would have looked so to you if you had been in a like fix."

———: : : :———

ANSWERS TO PRAYER

Once, when home for two or three days I was suffering pain in the region of my heart. At every beat it would seem to say, "Kelly, Kelly, Kelly." (Kelly was a place in North Dakota, about 260 miles from home. There were a few saints in the community who might be needing help). I was very sick and I told my wife how badly I was feeling. She said, "Perhaps the Lord wants you to go to Kelly." The next day the pain was still bothering me, so I sat down and wrote to O. O. Holman and said, "I am sick; if the pain in my heart does not soon stop I will be at your station Sunday at ten o'clock." This was in the month of August, the busy season for farmers. The pain did not stop, so I started out. When I had gone about one hundred miles from home the pain left me.

Having to change trains at Grand Forks and there being no train for Kelly until the next morning, I decided to go and stay over night with Brother C. H. Tubbs. At the parsonage I met Brother Newell, a minister, Brother Shave and Brother Niles, deacons of the congregation there, and a sister who was visiting.

They all exclaimed in surprise at seeing me appear at that time of the year and wanted to know the reason for my being there. I really felt sheepish about telling them. Kelly was only fifteen miles from Grand Forks and they had not heard of there being any serious trouble there.

After I had told them how I happened to be going to Kelly, Brother Tubbs turned to his wife and said, "Mary, you preach tomorrow; I want to go along with Bro. Susag and see what is going on." His wife said, "Charles, I am going along, too." Then to Bro. Newell he said, "You take the morning service tomorrow," but he also declined as he, too, wanted to go with us. And Bro. Shave made the same reply; he wanted to go to Kelly. But when Bro. Niles was asked to preach at the morning service, he kindly consented to take charge. In the morning I started out for Kelly with three ministers, one deacon and one sister accompanying me.

I am generally quite talkative, but I did not do much talking those fifteen miles, wondering what the people would think if, when getting there, we should find nothing unusual the matter. When the train stopped at the station I waited for all the folks to get off first. As I looked out of the window I saw Brother Holman standing on the platform weeping, looking at the people as they got off the train. Then I came. I went to him and asked him why he was weeping. He said, "We have been praying the Lord to send you to us and today I started for the station, confident that I would either meet you in person or that I would get a letter," and taking the letter from his pocket and holding it up, said, "and here I have both!" Then he told me that his wife was very ill, possibly dying, and that they had been praying the Lord to send me to them.

It was three miles out to their home in the country and Bro. Holman had only a one-seated buggy, so the two sisters drove and we preachers walked.

The good Lord heard prayer and healed Sister Holman. Also, an old lady of ninety years of age was baptized at this time.

———: : : : ———

On another occasion I was asked to come to Grand Forks to hold a revival meeting. On my arrival there I found that the pastor was having trouble with his eyes so that he had to stay at home in a dark room. Services started Friday night and it seemed that the whole congregation had become cooled off. This was made clear to me, so I preached three sermons—one on Friday night and two on Saturday. But it looked as though the condition grew worse instead of better as a result of my preaching.

Saturday night I had a dream. I dreamed that the Lord had sent me there to gather the sheep back that had wandered into a man's field and were tramping the grain down. Then I picked up one stone and threw it at them to try to get them back. I picked up another stone, and then threw the third one. They seemed now to be frightened worse than ever. This discouraged me and I said to the Lord, "What shall I do?" He said, "Speak gently to them."

Then I went into the field myself and called "Sheep!

Sheep!" to them, and they began to gather together and it wasn't long before I had a nice bunch of sheep up on the highway. I asked the Lord why it was I couldn't get them together without my going into the field myself, for I preached His word to them. "Yes," He said, "you preached My Word to them, **but it was the way you preached it.**" So Sunday I made my confession to the congregation and weeping, asked their forgiveness, and every one was brought back to the Lord, and a few sinners who were in the audience were also saved.

Through the week of services thirty-eight persons came from different states and Canada for healing — and there were some very serious cases. The night before the day we had set apart for the praying for the sick, I prayed from eleven o'clock that night until four o'clock in the morning in a dark room. When I got up from my knees the Lord stood before me and made it clear to me that He was going to heal every one of those who had been prayed for.

After all were healed and it was time for the services to close, a little nine year old girl came and sat on the altar bench. I went to her and said, "What do you want, Sophie?" In reply she said that she had seen how the Lord had healed the eyes of Sister Hobert and that now she wanted the Lord to heal her and set her eyes straight. (Her eyes were badly crossed).

On returning to the city some eight months later, I was invited to take supper with Brother and Sister Amondson, Sophie's parents. They had a number of children who came around me, and I wanted to know where the little girl was whose eyes were crossed and for whom I prayed several months before. A little girl spoke up and said, "Don't you know me? I am Sophie." I then asked her to tell me about her healing.

She told me that she was prayed for on that Friday night, and the following Monday she was starting out to school without her glasses and her mother, who was not saved, seeing her without her glasses, said, "Sophie, don't forget to wear your glasses!" Sophie answered, "Mother, I was prayed for at the revival meeting Friday night and I do not need my glasses." Her mother said, "Nonsense, come and get your glasses." But Sophie ran away to school!

That forenoon the teacher asked Sophie to read, and when she got up she said, "Sophie, haven't you your glasses with you?" (She knew Sophie had not been able to read without her glasses.) Sophie answered, lifting her hand, "Teacher, I was prayed for at the revival meeting Friday night and I do not need my glasses!" and her eyes were straight!

A number of years later I met Sophie with her little girl. She was a lovely looking woman and was happily married.

———: : : :———

I was baptizing a number of people in the North Sea, outside of Lokken, Denmark, among whom was Sister Swenborg, from Tiste, whose eyes were so crossed that she could not help herself at all without wearing her glasses. A big crowd was there, mocking and throwing sand at the saints. I had just baptized Sister Swenborg, and as she was coming out of the sea I heard a shout going up from the saints. They told me that as the sister was coming out of the water with lifted hands and looking up to heaven praising God, a halo of glory was shining around her head—and her eyes were straightened and she was a changed woman from that time. The mob stopped their mocking on seeing this demonstration.

After the service the next Sunday at Tiste, Sister Swenborg made the request that everybody meet her the next Tuesday afternoon at two-thirty o'clock at the boat landing as she had something of interest to tell them.

A big crowd gathered on Tuesday afternoon, and the sister climbed up on a large box holding her glasses in her hand and said to the people, "You all know me and my parents who live about six miles east of town. Before I was big enough to wear glasses it was necessary either for me to have someone lead me or to pull me in a little wagon or sleigh. I was saved recently in a meeting held by Bro. Morris C. Johnson and last week I went to Lokken and was baptized, and as I came out of the water my eyes were straightened. Here are my glasses," she said, holding them up and telling what they had cost, "Here they go! I don't need them anymore!" and into the sea they went. Then, opening her hand bag she took out a needle and said, "This is the finest needle on the market," and took thread and threaded it before the eyes of the astonished crowd.

———— : : : : ————

For a number of years I had suffered with appendicitis and during a meeting I was holding in company with Bro. Carl Arbeiter at Plum Coolie, Canada, I had a severe attack which lasted two days and two nights. The third night I was so tired and worn out that I went to sleep in spite of the pain. I woke up hearing myself say, "Don't stick that knife into me." The appendix was swollen to about the size of a small hen's egg, and I felt it was going to burst. There was no time to get anyone to come and pray so I laid my own hands on my body and said, "Lord God Almighty, if you do not help me now I am gone." It burst, making a noise like the shot from a small shotgun. I then turned over to my other side and went to sleep at once and have never experienced any bad effects nor had any attacks since.

In relating this experience to three doctors later, two of them laughed and made fun of me, but the third one said, "Hold on, hold on; this man has never lied to me yet." He said it could have burst into the intestines, the poison passing out the natural way. And if not, the Lord God could take care of him!

———: : : :———

Once I had a stroke. Half the left side of my body down to my knees was affected. I could not sit up, neither could I lie down. I stood on my knees beside the sofa for two weeks. I was prayed for several times but was not healed. And I was to start a revival meeting at Hereford, Minn. the Thursday of the second week that I was sick.

Sister Hedricks came over often and prayed for me. When on the second Friday she came and I was no better, she asked me whether I had sent to Anderson and to the Scandinavian Publishing Company at St. Paul Park to have them pray for me. On telling her I had not done so and explaining to her that I had no faith for my own healing, I said, "I could pray for your healing if you were sick, but I have no faith for myself, and I have always preached that when folks were saved they should have faith to pray for their own healing, so I do not want to bother the folks to pray for me." "Well," she said, "aren't you humble enough to tell them that you have no faith for yourself?" I answered, "All right, you pray for me and I will think it over." The next day I asked wife to write to these two places, and when she had written and sealed the two letters I was instantly healed! Wife sent the letters.

After getting healed I decided to go to the revival

Personal Experiences of S. O. Susag

meeting at Hereford, but there was no train going there until Monday and it was in the month of November and very cold. And it was at the time when the automobile first came into use. One family in the congregation at Hereford had a Ford furnished with a top and side curtains, another family had a Buick (called a gentleman's car), and it had no top nor even a windshield on it.

I found out later that the owning of these cars had caused some little friction in the congregation. In fact, some had said that nobody could have one of those machines and still be a Christian. But they had decided to leave the matter until the time Brother Susag should come and he would help them out.

When we were leaving my home to drive to town to take the train for there, it was really cold. I said to my wife, "Let's go back in the house and ask the Lord to send a man to meet me at Elbow Lake, with a car having a top on it and side curtains"—for I was still very weak. On arriving at Elbow Lake I went to the post office and wrote a card home—I would have had to change trains there if no one had come to meet me—and as I came out of the post office I saw a man across the street walking in the direction I was going. He looked at me and I looked at him, wondering, then he came running across the street and exclaimed, "Now I know why I came to town today! I am here to drive you to the meeting. I had left my car in town to have a little work done on it, not intending to use it until after the meeting."

Then he went on to say, "We live six miles from town, and this morning as I was working around the barn the Lord said to me, 'You go to town and get your car.' My wife said, 'John, leave that car alone; don't go to town.' But I told her that the Lord said, 'You go and get the car.'

And I came as fast as I could get here."

He took me to the service. Bro. E. G. Masters was preaching, and when he had finished speaking he asked me to come to the pulpit and tell how the Lord had healed me and how it was that I managed to get to the service. I related the whole story, telling how I had prayed for someone to meet me who had a car having a top to it and side curtains to keep out the cold. I then added that I was so glad the Lord had lots of cars; that as for me, I never expected to have a car of my own for I did not think that I would ever be able to afford anything like that. That settled the car difficulty in the congregation—and I was entirely ignorant of the fact of there having been any trouble! Today I am using my ninth car.

That meeting was a real success. Brother Masters, for a number of evenings, had offered a brand new eighteen dollar Bible to any preacher, professor, presiding elder or bishop that could come into the pulpit and prove that we were not preaching the Bible. He gave them five minutes to come to the front. One family belonging to a certain denomination sent for their bishop and he came. After the service was over and the family had taken the bishop to their home, they asked him why he did not get up and prove that we were not preaching the truth so as to get the Bible. The good man answered, "After those two men were finished speaking there was nothing to say. They preached the Bible." Brother Masters spoke on the "White Horse of Calvary" and used the blackboard to illustrate his meaning.

———: : : :———

Brother Peter Peterson of Hoboken, New Jersey and I held some meetings together up in a newly settled district of northern Minnesota. Our offering for two weeks services was one round fifty-cent piece.

While there we had a call to go to the insane asylum at Fergus Falls, Minnesota to pray for a Brother Weegan who had lost his mind. After entering the institution we were locked in the cell with him and on bended knees with our hands uplifted toward heaven, we began to pray and all of a sudden he was restored to his right mind. We knocked on the door to have the attendant came and let us out. As we were going out of the door Brother Weegan pushed his head between us and the attendant and said to the man, "You might just as well let me out, too, for I am as rational as these two preachers now, and I will not hurt you any more."

Then I asked the attendant whether there was a man in the place by the name of John Lukesen of Irving, Minn., and he told me there was such a man there. I told him we had ten minutes to spare and asked him whether we could go in and see him without first having to go to the superintendent's office for permission. The man lifted his hands and said, "You can see anyone in this institution since this one man has received help from you."

He then proceeded to give us information about the one we wanted to see. He said, "When Mr. Lukesen first came here we had to have him in a padded cell and he got so bad that we had to tie him to his cot and now he is like a wild cat and nothing but skin and bones; he won't be long for this world."

When he opened the door to the cell, there I saw my neighbor lying on his cot and he surely did look like a wild cat, as the man had said! The compassion of the Lord Jesus came upon me and I lifted my hands toward heaven and called aloud to him, "John Lukesen, the Lord Jesus Christ, whom I serve, makes you well!" And HE WAS WELL! Shortly after this, he was sent home.

We planned to go from there to Hereford, Minnesota. At Evansville where we had to change trains, we inquired of the station agent when the train for Hereford would be leaving. We were informed that there would be no train leaving for that place before Thursday at three o'clock. We were told that only two trains a week went from there to Hereford and this was Tuesday—a long time to wait!

Brother Peterson said, "Let us go out and pray." After we had prayed we returned to the depot and asked the agent when the train for Hereford would be leaving. He answered gruffly, "I told you Thursday afternoon at three o'clock." "All right," said Brother Peterson, "Let us go out and pray." After praying we went back the second time and asked the agent the same question; and this time he was really gruff. And he surely informed us that there would be no train leaving before Thursday afternoon at three o'clock. Again, Brother Peterson said, "All right, let us go out and pray."

We went out once more into the grove to pray and Brother Peterson did the praying: "Lord, the President can get a special pullman train any time he wants it and he is only the president of the United States; and here are we, Brother Susag and I, Thy ambassadors. We are not asking Thee for a pullman car—we will be satisfied with an old caboose—the distance is only 30 miles; so Lord, won't you please talk to the agent?" We both said AMEN.

On returning to the agent for the third time, Brother Peterson said to him, "When will that train be ready for Hereford?" In a very mild tone he replied, "I have been thinking about it and I will shove a few box cars and a caboose together and send you fellows out." And we both said, "Thank you, sir." And so the Lord answered prayer and sent us home on a special train!

When wife and I got saved, my brothers and families and wives quit writing to us, and in four years we seldom heard from them. One evening a letter came from my sister-in-law telling us that my brother had lost his reason and had been sent to the insane asylum at St. Peter, Minn., and asking me to come at once. Not having any money on hand to go with, I went to a near neighbor and showed him the letter and asked him if he would loan me fifteen dollars so that I could go to Minneapolis and also to St. Peter. He told me that he would do that even if I were not able to pay him back. The next day I went to Minneapolis to my sister-in-law and her five children. Jerome, the oldest boy, seven years of age, said, "Uncle, are you going to bring Daddy home?" I said, "Son, I cannot bring your Daddy home, but Jesus Christ whom I serve will bring him home."

My sister-in-law related how it all happened. She went for her pastor and my brother-in-law, a professor in the Lutheran college. When they came Jerome said to them, "Won't you pray like Uncle Swen does?" They had evidently talked about our praying even though they did not write to us. After they had gone his wife had to let my brother out-doors and he ran four blocks without a thread of clothing on—until a policeman captured him.

I went to St. Peter, and Dr. Tumbleson, the president of the institution, refused to let me see my brother. I told him that I must see him; that as a minister of the gospel I had a right to go where a doctor could go. But he still refused and called in two other doctors who said to me, "Your brother is not only insane but is seriously ill and we do not expect him to leave this institution alive." To which I replied, "Then so much the more do I have to see him; and if you continue to refuse to let me see him you will have two Susags in this institution, for I will stay until you grant me the right to see my brother." Finally relenting, they sent for a man to take me to see my poor brother.

As I entered the cell in which he was confined my brother did not know me. He was walking around the room more like an animal than like a man. I knelt down in the middle of the floor and prayed. After a while he came and put his hand on my shoulder and said, "Swen, how does it come that you are here?" I said, "I have come to help you, Mike." "Thank you, I am glad you have come; something got into my head and I lost my mind. How is my family?" I told him they were all well and had sent their greetings to him. Then the man who had brought me in took hold of me and ordered me out.

But I was satisfied. This was the 22nd of March and I fasted from one meal every day for seventeen days and some days I would touch neither water nor food telling the Lord I had promised Mike's wife and his children that I was going to bring the husband and daddy home; and, "Jesus, I will give you no rest until you do so."

On the eighth of April during morning worship the Spirit of the Lord revealed to me that the Lord had heard our prayer and that my brother was perfectly well! I jumped up from my knees and ran around the house shouting the glory of God. Wife thought, "Here is another crazy Susag," but Brother Enos Key, of Red Key, Indiana (who had come to hold a meeting) was with us and he said, "Praise God, Brother Susag has the victory!" And three days later I received a letter from Doctor Tumbleson giving us the good news that on the eighth day of April the nurse went to take food to my brother and found him perfectly well in mind and body. And that he was doing bookkeeping for the institution and could come home any time only for the customary red tape it would take a few days before he could come. In a short time he was home and well.

::::

On one occasion when I was holding a meeting at the fishing town of Sookden, Denmark, a great storm arose. As is the custom in fishing towns, boats put out to sea at high tide for better fishing conditions; forty-two had gone from here about two o'clock in the night. Toward morning the storm broke and on into the forenoon it became very fierce. Some of the older people were telling of a similar storm they remembered of some forty years before when thirty-eight boats went out and such a storm blew up. If I remember correctly, not one boat returned.

In those days there were no motor boats. They were all sailboats, generally three men to a boat. This time, however, they had gasoline motors on the boats and from twelve o'clock until three o'clock one boat after the other returned, some of them full of water, barely getting to shore. Forturnately the wind was blowing toward the shore or they might not have made a safe landing.

I was staying at the home of Brother Morton Petersen. He and his crew had not returned as yet. It seemed that most of the population of the town was standing on the hills looking for his return. I heard someone say to his wife, "Marie, do you expect Morton to return?" She answered, "He has been out so many times and has come back, and I expect him back this time." He generally went farther out than any of the fishermen because the farther out the fish were supposed to be larger and better.

We stood out there for two hours or more. About five o'clock someone said, "I see a dark spot out there." A little later someone else shouted, "I see a spot, too!" And then we began to see the spot more and more often, and at last they came safely to land—and not a bucket of water in the boat.

On our way home I asked Brother Petersen how he had gotten along. He said, "When we realized the storm was on hand we packed up our fishing lines and I ordered my partner to take care of the motor and I myself took charge of the rudder. My partner was a saved man but we had a boy who was not saved. I ordered him to be ready to dip out the water if any got in the boat."

I asked him whether they did much talking during that terrible storm and he said, "No, I was praying all the time that we might reach land safely, because the young man with us was not saved and he was the sole support of his widowed mother, his father and one or two brothers having gone down somewhere in the North Sea not so long ago. We were getting along very well—for the Lord helped me steer the boat right—but the worst that we had to meet was just before we landed—there were three sandbars we had to cross. If the waves struck us just right we would get over, but if not, we would get stuck in the sandbars, and there would be no help for us. When we came to the first one a big wave carried us safely over the sandbar. I said 'Thank God, we are over the first one;' and so it was with the other two; and each time I said, 'Thank God for taking us over, and too, for not letting the water get into our boat.' "

A week later I embarked on the steamer **Olaf Barger,** sailing from Fredriksen, Denmark, to Sweden. As I was going on board the boat the Captain came to me and asked whether I could spare him a few minutes before we landed in Sweden, as he wished to have a talk with me. When we got so far that we could begin to see the rocky coast of Sweden he came to me and began his narrative. He said, pointing ahead, "You see that three-mast schooner standing upon that rock?" I said, "Yes, I see it." "You remember the awful storm we had a week ago today. We were just coming out from Gottenburg to return to Denmark—an hour's sailing—and the schooner called for help but we were unable to even help ourselves so that we could not possibly help them. They were blown upon the rocks, but the people were saved." Then he pointed to the left to two big rocks, and continued, "And right there was a small steamer in trouble. They, too, called for help but we could not give it and they went down.

"We now saw that it would be impossible for us to reach Denmark and were fortunate in managing to turn the ship's course back toward Gottenburg. I tied myself to the bridge with an inch rope. Down into the waves we went and I said to myself, "We have seen the sun for the last time." But we came up and went down again many, many times. Then I did something I had never in all my life done before—I am sixty-five years old—I prayed the Lord to save my ship and all that were sailing with me. Along in the afternoon I found myself calling on God for salvation of my soul, and the Lord did save me and finally brought my ship, and those sailing with me, safely into the harbor at nine o'clock that evening, it having taken us nine hours to do one hour's sailing."

"Knowing that you were a minister of the gospel I wanted to tell you the story that you might perhaps tell it to others."

How longsuffering and merciful is the Son of God toward the children of men that when they repent and turn to Him, HE FORGIVES THEM.

———— : : : : ————

One time when I arrived home from one of my evangelistic tours I found that my two young sons who were twins, eleven years of age, had been cutting hay. It was all raked and rowed up ready for hauling, and they were rejoicing that I had come as they were counting on me to help them haul and stack the hay. They said, "Dad, tomorrow you will have to help us." I said, "All right, we will have to get up early to get it done as I am leaving the following day to start another meeting."

The next morning we started out. We had to drive eighty rods south on the road, then we turned another eighty rods east to the hay meadow. Just as I began to pitch the hay up in the rack the boys exclaimed, "Dad, it's raining." "Yes," I said, and stuck my pitchfork in the ground, threw my hat beside it and said, "Let's pray." I said to the Lord, "This hay is yours; this farm is yours and I am your servant. This hay must be hauled today as I leave tomorrow to minister unto the people, so please, at least keep the rain off the hay meadow and off the road where we have to drive. Amen."

I went to pitching hay again; it was just pouring down all around us as far as we could see across the fence and west of the road. The only spots where it did not rain was where we were working and on the road we were driving. It rained all day, and it did not just RAIN—IT POURED! We hauled hay all day, until a little after six o'clock I slid off the stack in the yard and then the rain just poured down. I said to the boys, "The Lord surely heard prayer." They said, "Yes, He did," and we thanked the Lord.

After I had left the next day, our neighbor came over and seeing the stack asked the boys when they stacked that hay. They told him, "Yesterday, Daddy was home." (There was a distance of about twenty rods between his house and ours). He said, "That is impossible. I took a rest all day for the rain just poured down and I could not do anything." He thought it must have been the day before that we hauled and stacked the hay. But the boys told him that "Daddy prayed and it did not rain on our hay meadow, nor on the road where we were driving." This man was greatly astonished at hearing this.

———— : : : : ————

One afternoon, about three o'clock, the renters on our place came running in great excitement into wife's room and said, "Mrs. Susag, a cyclone is coming." She went out with them and it was dark. There was a wood pile about three or four rods south of our houses and parts of our neighbors buildings south of us were blowing through our pasture and wood from the wood pile began to go up in the air. Wife lifted her hands toward heaven facing the storm and cried, "Lord God, don't let that storm strike our dwelling." The cyclone turned right square to the east several rods and then turned square again to the north—east of the buildings. When it got beyond our buildings it turned west and when it got just in line with the direction from which it came, it turned north again, rooting up big trees and damaging the neighbor's buildings; but not a thing on our premises was disturbed.

The spout of the cyclone dug a ditch several feet deep in some places. Once more God's Word was verified: "Call and I will answer."

———— : : : : ————

GLUTTONOUS MAN WITH DYSPEPSIA

At a meeting we were holding, Brother Tubbs, Brother Enos Key and myself was asked to fast and pray for a man weighing from 250 to 260 pounds and calling himself a saint!

We fasted, accordingly, and went after service Sunday noon to pray for him. We were still fasting, but he sat up to the table and ate a big chicken dinner and when he had finished eating he said, "Now you can pray for me." Bro. Tubbs said, "No, we are not going to pray for you. We have been fasting for you, and still haven't eaten, and you have sat up to the table and eaten as much as we three preachers, together, could eat. Goodbye!" And out we went.

——— : : : : ———

CASTING OUT DEVILS

At a meeting in Chicago there was a woman possessed with devils, and wanted to be delivered. Seven ministers, four men and three sisters, were working with her for over an hour but without apparent success. We tried to lay our hands on her but the devils in her would kick our hands away. Big knots came out on her body, on her shoulders and neck the size of a good sized apple. Then we ministers withdrew for a consultation among ourselves—to see whether the hindering cause in casting these devils out, lay in us, among ourselves—to be assured of complete unity and agreement in our midst: And we found that there was perfect unity. That being the case, we said, "We must have the victory, the evil spirits must go." We went back to the woman and worked, prayed and rebuked the enemy for nearly three hours, all to no avail.

Then one brother said, "There must be someone in the chapel sympathizing with her." We began a search looking everywhere to find where the trouble was and behind some folding doors in the prayer room we found a man. Brother Knight said to him, "What are you doing here?" He said, "Can't I stay here?" But he was told to leave forthwith and he went. We then locked the doors of the chapel and in a few minutes the woman was delivered.

She was obliged to go home as her husband went to work at four o'clock in the morning, but he came back the next day and was gloriously saved.

Another case of demon possession happened in Grand Forks. During a meeting we were holding there, a man came to the service who formerly had taken his stand with the church, coming out of a certain denomination, but before long he returned to it again. When he came to the meeting we were holding he was possessed. In one of the services Brother Krutz and I attempted to lay hands on him: He was kneeling at the altar with his back to the pulpit and he was taken up bodily and thrown upon the rostrum against the wall behind the pulpit. I ran after him and the devil said to me, "Now, it will go with you as it did with the seven sons of Sceva." I rebuked the devil and when I got to the man he turned over on his back and slid, head first, off the rostrum toward the seats, knocking his head against the seats until it seemed as though his skull would surely be broken.

I called for help. Eight brothers came and held him so that he would not get hurt. We laid hands on him and commanded the evil spirits to come out of him but they did not come. Then I asked them, "What is your name?" The answer was, "Salvation Army devil." Then in the name of the Lord Jesus we commanded the salvation army devil to come out of him. And when they went out it was with such a horrible scream that many women jumped up on their seats in fright and the man's shirt was torn and blood was running from his mouth and he fell on the floor as though he were dead. We let him lie there a little while, then laying our hands on him, prayed and he came to. This man repented, made his confession and was saved.

———:::: ———

Bro. Drysdale of Grand Forks, who had a stiff knee, was prayed for several times, but got no help. However, in this meeting his limb became so limbered up that he could run up and down the steps like a young man. He got so happy that he forgot his cane and went home without it. On getting home he discovered he had left his cane behind and ran back to the chapel to get it, but when he got hold of his cane, his limb was as bad as ever.

When I was in Minneapolis with Brother E. G. Masters, a lady came to us to be prayed for. She was walking with two canes. She was prayed for and the Lord healed her. And she got around like a young woman. She went home forgetting to take her two canes—and they were beautiful canes! She came back to get them, but when she got hold of them she was just as crippled as ever, and no praying helped her.

——— : : : : ———

One time I was asked by the congregation at Rice Lake, Wisconsin, to come and hold a meeting for them. And I felt that the Lord wanted me to do so. I wrote the pastor there about it four times a year for two years, but he did not want me. However the Lord said, "You go," and I went. On my arrival at Rice Lake, I found the pastor sick in bed.

I said to him, "Well, I'm here now; the Lord told me to come." He told me the chapel was open and that I should go ahead. I started that meeting with eight to twelve school children and two women coming to the services, keeping on for two weeks. Many times the devil said to me, "So you thought the Lord sent you, didn't you? Now you see . . .!"

The last Sunday night, to cap the climax, the children came around me and said, "Reverend, aren't you going to close the services?" I asked, "Do you want them to close?" They said they did. I asked them the reason and they said, "We like your preaching so much better than our pastors, but we go to school and we get so tired from coming every night." Then I said to them, "Children, your reason is very good. But what do you think of this proposition: that we announce services for Monday, Tuesday and Wednesday evenings, and if no more come we will close the meeting and you tell your folks about it?" The children thought it would be fine.

The next night, Monday, two more women came and they came the next night too, and one of them (if not both of them) got saved. But what happened the next two evenings is erased from my memory, but Friday evening when I came to open the door for the service, there were more people than there was room in the chapel to accommodate them. So they stood around on boxes and ladders outside the windows. Fifty-two were at the altar for salvation in the last three weeks—I was there five weeks in all. The last Saturday I went to the pastors home and said to him, "I have come to pray for you. You are going to get healed today so you can attend the service tomorrow. But you will have to come early or you will not be able to get into your own pulpit." He broke down and cried and said, "I haven't a pair of decent trousers to wear to stand before such a big audience." I said, "I have two pairs, thank God, I will give you one pair." I prayed for him and he was healed.

At a later time Brother Masters and I held another meeting there. One evening a couple came in a little late and sat down in the back seat. This was the first time they had attended the service and they got under conviction, but they got out before we could get to speak to them. They came the next evening and slipped out again before we could get to them. They did not come any more. We began to inquire around to find out their names and where they lived. Yes, we were informed, he was a real estate agent, and they never go to church anywhere. We went to their home and had a fine visit with them one afternoon for about two hours. They were nice folks. Brother Masters said, "We have not seen you out to the services any more since the second time you were there." "Well," they said, we are not in the habit of going to any meetings, but we enjoyed the beautiful singing so much the first night that we decided we would go again the next evening.

We didn't want to be late, so I decided to milk our cow after service. After coming home from the service I took my lantern, as we have not any light in the barn and hung it up on a nail on the studding and went to milking. As the milk began to run I heard a noise like a shot and the lantern went out, leaving me in total darkness. When I went to examine what had happened, it appeared that I had been so disturbed in my mind over what I heard at the services that I had made a mistake and had hung the milk pail up instead of the lantern and when the milk began to drop on the lantern-globe it broke." "Well," we said, "you are coming to the services again?" But they answered, "We surely are not. If two services can affect us to such an extent as nearly cause us to lose our minds we will never go back again. We only go to the funeral services of our neighbors."

———: : : :———

At one time when I was in Denmark, I was in dire need of a considerable sum of money. I prayed earnestly over the matter and one day as I went to put my hat on my head it seemed to be too small. I took it off and looked on the inside of it to be sure it was mine and in feeling around, on the inside of the sweat band I found the very amount of money I needed.

———— : : : : ————

While still in Denmark, I needed an overcoat. I went to a clothing store and picked out one. There were a few alterations to be made and I was to get it in two or three days, but I had no money and did not know from where any was coming. This was Friday and Sunday evening after service a number of saints went passed my door and one sister threw a folded bill on to my table. She said, "Brother Susag, you need an overcoat. Here is a little to help on it." I thanked her and looked at the bill and found it was a hundred crown bill—more than seven crowns over the cost of the overcoat.

———— : : : : ————

Once when I was in Grand Forks holding a meeting, my oldest son wrote me that a man to whom I owed $27.50 needed $20.00 and that if I could pay the twenty he would give $7.50. Between the forenoon service and that of the afternoon, I stayed in the church to pray and just before the next service was to begin a number of people came in and stood beside the stove warming themselves. An elderly woman from South Dakota put out her hand to me and said, "Praise the Lord, Brother Susag," and putting a crumpled bill into my hand, said, "This is for you." I thanked her and went behind the pulpit and thanked the Lord for twenty dollars and when I looked at it, it was twenty dollars.

The next day, between morning and afternoon services, I took a walk and on my way I passed a fruit stand. As

I looked into the window of it I saw some delicious red apples, and Oh, how I wished I had three of them. I went back three times and looked at them, but I had no money. I went back to the chapel and the same old sister that had given me the twenty dollars the day before, handed me a little paper bag and in it, to my happy surprise, were three of those delicious apples that I had wanted.

One time when I was in Denmark, I wanted to go from Hjoremg to Lokkum. I did not have the money for my carfare but stood up against a pillar in the station praying the Lord to send it. As it was getting near train time it looked as though it were not coming when suddenly a lady whom I knew—she was not saved—came into the depot and crossed right over to me and handed me a five crown bill. This lady had heard me often tell of the Lord hearing prayer, but she did not believe that it was all true. I took it hastily, ran for the ticket window, purchased my ticket and was just in time to catch the train. When I came back, this lady came to the services and when I saw her I asked her whether I had thanked her for the bill she had given me at the depot. She said, "No, you didn't have time. When I came in to the depot and saw you standing there, something said to me, 'He's praying for carfare; go, give him five crowns,' and when I gave it to you I saw tears in your eyes and when I got home I knelt down and asked the Lord to save me and He did." Then she said, "You were praying for carfare, weren't you?" I assured her I surely was. "God moves in a mysterious way, His wonders to perform."

———: : : : ———

At the first Camp meeting we held, I went to the bank and borrowed ten dollars to divide among the ministers, and one day the Lord said to me, "Give Elihu Key five dollars."

I couldn't understand so went to wife and told her about it; she said, "If the Lord told you to give Brother Key five dollars, you had better give it to him; he must be needing it badly." So the next day I crumpled a five dollar bill up and stuck it in his hand. He said, "Thank you," and into the brush he went—and I went after him, crawling on my hands and knees so he would not see me—quite close up to him. He fell on his knees, crying and thanking the Lord for the five dollars and for the man who gave it to him and asking the Lord to bless him a hundred-fold according to His word. Then down the hill he ran to the Post Office and sent it to his family. This I learned later from his brother. The family was in great need.

——— : : : : ———

On one occasion a payment of $245.00 had to be made on the contracts on our home—to save the contract from lapsing. I did not have the money. I tried every possible way to borrow it from different banks, and failing that, I tried to get it from some of the brethren. The last one I approached surely capped the climax. He assured me that he had the money and could loan it to me, but he said that he might just as well throw the money on the manure pile, for, he said, "You can never pay for the place anyhow, and the quicker you leave it the better."

I went home, and after praying for three days the Lord said the name "Torp" to me. The only one I knew of that name was a banker in Willmer, our county seat, whom I had met once—he hardly knew me nor I him. Anyway, I went to him and told him my trouble, to which he responded by saying that he could not loan me any money; that I was out of the district for him to loan on chattel mortgages; that I would either have to get it at Paynesville, Atwater or New

London. I told him that I had already applied at those places but could not obtain the loan. Then Mr. Torp asked me what security I was able to give, to which I replied that the security I had would not be worth fifty dollars, but that I had a strong back and two strong arms and a good will and that we would like to stay on the hill a little longer if it were at all possible. He said, "Such things will go a long way." He sat there silent for a minute or two, then he said, "I'll think the matter over and you come back after dinner." A lump got into my throat so that I could not even say, "Thank you."

I walked down into the railroad yards, found a place between two box cars and prayed for nearly an hour and a half—back and forth I went praying that the Lord would "speak to the dear man and make his heart tender toward this poor man and his family." I went back to the bank and the good man met me. He invited me into his office, and when we were seated he said, "I have thought the matter over and I am going to loan you the money; now what security have you to offer?" I said, "I have a bay colt, a couple of calves, an old wagon I paid seven dollars for, and some other little trinkets." "Well," he said, "the colt as it grows will increase in price—good horses at that time were only worth about fifty dollars—and the calves also will increase in value. How long a time do you want?" I told him I thought eight months. Then he told me that their charge for such loans was 12%, but that he would let me have it for 8%.

Three weeks before the note came due I went to see him. My purpose in going was in regard to the loan. "Well," he said, "it is not due yet; we have not sent you a notice." I told him that I was wanting to know whether he would extend the time on the note. He asked me whether I had anything at all to pay on it. I told him I had only $50.00 and the interest. To which he replied, "That's fine." (It took me two years instead of eight months to pay off the loan; but I was always on hand ahead of time to get the extension. When I made the last payment he gave me one dollar.

I went to see this banker some years later, and I asked him what it was that had made him so kind to me. Tears came into his eyes, but he did not answer—and my eyes were moist as well. He turned and from a drawer took out a small tract in which was an account of his boyhood life and experiences. His father died when he was eleven years old. He took a job as ship boy on board a ship and went through untold hardships to help support his mother and his six brothers and sisters. When he was about seventeen he came to America and located in Wisconsin.

When the Civil War was on a certain rich man came to him with an offer of several hundred dollars if he would act as substitute for his son in the army—which offer, however, he refused. Some time later he became acquainted with a family in which were seven children who were very good to him. One day word came that the father, who was a soldier, was killed in action and that the oldest boy was to be taken to fill his father's place. Whereupon young Torp stepped up to the boy and said, "You go home and take care of your mother and the family and I will go in your place—free of charge. The Lord was good to him and protected him; very soon he was promoted to the rank of an officer — and so the booklet continued, telling of his life's experiences.

These two incidents remind me, by way of contrast, of the story of another banker and of the way he dealt with a poor man who was in debt to him. When not prepared to meet the payments on his note the poor man would ask for an extension of time. Finally the banker became impatient and refused to grant any further time extension. The poor man begged for mercy—that he would allow him more time. "All right," said the banker, "I have a glass eye; it is such a good one that people cannot tell which one it is; if you can tell which one, I will extend the loan." Looking carefully at the eyes the man said, "It is the left one." "Yes," said the other, "how could you tell?" The man said, "I could tell that eye was more sympathetic than the good one." It is said of Jesus that he "learned obedience through the things that he suffered"—and so with us, we learn how to have sympathy according to how we suffer.

――― : : : : ―――

My first experience of being healed of cancer of the stomach was while I was in Grand Forks in 1922 after that Doctor Weatherstein had examined me and said there was nothing that could be done for me. I was taken to the Werstlein's home where I was staying, and Brother Shave, Sister Gaulke and Sister Johnstone were sent for. They came, and when they saw me as I lay on the lounge, they fell on their knees weeping and calling on God. All at once they arose, and with Sister Werstlein, laid their hands on me and rebuked the devil AND THE CANCER, and I was instantly healed!

In the fall of 1936 I had a number of calls to go to the West Coast, but I did not feel that I could leave unless wife had someone to stay with her. However, she insisted that I should go, saying she was able to take care of herself, but I hesitated about going so far away and applied for a job as an automobile adjuster paying $50 a week and commission. I had everything signed up on Friday, and I was to go to work the following Tuesday. On Sunday the cancer returned again for the third time—the blood running from me and I was very sick. Wife said—not in an unkind way—"Good enough for you." I said, "I know what you are going to say." "Yes," she went on, "but I will check up on you. Do you remember what Brother Dorrity said to you when you were ordained? 'This is not for a day, nor for a week, nor for a month or a year, but for your lifetime,' and you are not dead yet!" To which I replied, suffering and weeping, "All right, you come and pray for me." She came and prayed and I was instantly healed. Needless to say, I did not take the job.

This took place the Sunday before Thanksgiving. On Thanksgiving day we were to go by invitation to Willmar to dinner and in the evening we were to attend service and I was to preach. That was the last automobile trip my wife ever took with me.

In the same year we were living on our little farm. On December the first, as I was going to town, wife made out a little list of things she wanted me to buy, but in spite of the list I forgot two of the items I was to get—and they were never purchased for they were never needed. On Monday the 8th I said to her, "Perhaps I had better go to town and get those two articles," but she said, "Never mind, we will wait until someone else goes in."

Being clerk of the district school board and her brother the chairman, when he came over, they talked over some business matters and other affairs that evening. The next morning she got up early. I saw a light in her room and I asked her whether she was getting up. She said she was; so I thought I had better go down and stir up the fire. When she came down she said, "If you want a job you can get breakfast ready." I answered, "Okay, what do you want to eat?" She said, "A glass of milk, a slice of toast and a soft cooked egg." Then she said, "I suppose you want oatmeal!" I said, "Sure."

After breakfast we had our morning worship and then she went to read and write. After I had washed the dishes I said, "I am going to town to get those two articles." To which she replied, "It is up to you. No hurry about it." I went out to the garage to get the car and found I had a flat tire, so I went back into the house and said, "It is cold out there and there is a flat tire." She said, "Never mind."

About eleven o'clock she put her hands up to her ears and said, "I have such pain around my ears." Then she went over to the sofa and lay down, but the pain grew worse. I went to her and knelt down; we prayed and she was instantly made well.

At noon I fixed a little lunch, after which I said, "Now I will go and fix the tire and go to town." She laughed and said, "So now you are going to be a man again."

I jacked up the car but could not turn any of the bolts on the wheel. I walked to the neighbor's and borrowed a coal chisel but still I could not move a bolt even with the hammer and chisel. All at once I heard a rattle as though someone was dying. It startled me. I threw down the hammer and chisel, and ran for the house like a wild man, jerking open one door after another, and slamming them as I went. When I opened the last one, there I saw wife sitting in the rocker reading, and she laughed. I raised my hands and said to her, "You are not dead yet!" She answered, "I should say not! I was wondering what kind of a cowboy had come rattling through the house!"

Then I told her that I could not get the wheel off. After a few minutes she said, "Uncle Carl (her brother) said to me, 'Martha, why don't you take a rest? You are always so busy and you don't have to keep going like that,' so now I am going up stairs to take a rest. You come with me and carry my Bible and a few other things." So I went with her. After I had tucked her in bed I asked her if she was resting comfortably now. She said, "Yes," and looking up at me with a smile, she said, as though she was about to tell me a secret, "And now . . ."—and she was dead! I raised my hands and said, "O Mama, you are not leaving me, are you?" But there she lay smiling.

I called the doctor and in a few minutes the house was full of people. The first one to come was Sister Hansen. She said, "Brother Susag, Sister Susag is not dead — she lies there smiling!" But she was gone. She had been praying for about two years that she might go that way, and her prayer was answered. (I got a neighbor young man to come and see what he could do with the car. He had no trouble in turning the bolts and was able to fix it very easily.) The feeling I had that I could not leave my wife to go to the West Coast to hold meetings proved to have been quite in order.

———:::::———

On one of my trips I had to change trains at Grand Forks, and having a little time to spare I walked down a certain street of the city and met Brother John Sonden who was standing outside of a doctor's office. He was surprised to see me, but I explained that I was just passing through in making my train connections. He said he was waiting for his son, Brent, who was up in the office consulting the doctor about his health. He wished so much that I could talk to the boy. At his request I went and met him as he was coming out of the consulting room.

He informed me that the doctor had told him he had heart trouble, but as he did not know what kind, he wanted him to go to the hospital for a week when he thought he would be able to locate the ailment. After hearing what he had to say, I said to him, "I'll tell you what your trouble is and how you feel when you are sitting on the gang plow, plowing: You feel you are going to fall off in front of the plow and get killed and that makes you nervous and sick." He said, "Yes sir, that is exactly how I feel." I then said to him, "I can tell you the cure for it: Go home, and falling on your knees, confess your sins to God and call on Him for salvation. I will be agreed in prayer and I guarantee you will be well—and now, goodbye, Brent, I must run to catch my train."

A year later when driving past his farm with Brother Holman, I saw a man out in the field and asked Brother Holman whether that was Brent Sonden. He said it was, and out of the car I got and ran over to him in the field saying, "Praise the Lord, Brent—did you follow the advice I gave you a year ago?" He answered, "Yes, and I have never had that feeling again since the Lord saved me."

———— : : : : ————

At one time I went to Hereford, Minnesota to preach for Brother George Green while he went on a trip to Iowa. At the Sunday morning service I learned that Elder Larson had met with an automobile accident the night before, breaking his left arm in two places and had been taken to the hospital at Barrett. His father phoned me that he would call for me and take me with him to the hospital.

On our arrival there, we found three doctors on the spot ready to amputate the arm—they were to take it off between the shoulder and the elbow. But I protested, saying, "That arm is not going to be amputated; those bones have to be set; for if you take the arm off you can never put it back again." But the doctors objected, "That is all we can do." I replied, "If Doctor Phelon of Paynesville had been at home I would have called for him to come and he would have fixed those bones in a jiffy." They replied, "We know him and he is no better than we are."

They turned to the father and said, "Are you going to listen to us or to this old foggy preacher?" "Well," he answered, "The old minister knows something too." At this, two of the doctors picked up their instruments and left. The one remaining said to me, "What are you going to do?" I said, "I am going to Hereford to preach tonight, after which I'll come back and take the young man with me on the train to Minneapolis." "But," he said, "gangrene may set in." I told him that I would pray God Almighty to keep that away. Then he asked me whether I was going alone with the boy, and I told him I was. He said that I was a brave man, but I answered, "No, it is not that I am brave, but that young man would give anything to have his two arms." Then the doctor said, "How would it be if I were to go with you?" I told him that it would be fine. When we were on the train he asked me where I was going to take the young man when we got to Minneapolis. I told him I hadn't thought of that, but in a city of 500,000 people there must be a doctor capable of setting bones. If not, I said, "I'll do it myself." "All right," replied the doctor, "We'll take him to the Fairview Hospital; I know a doctor there who is good at setting bones. His name is Seversen." And this we decided to do.

It was early when we arrived in the city, so we first had breakfast, after which I was introduced to Dr. Seversen. I said to him, "So you are the doctor who is going to set the bones in that arm?" But he said, "It can't be done; the arm will have to be amputated." I said, "That suggestion has been made to me before, and that arm is not going to come off." While we were talking several other doctors had come in—some thirteen or fourteen in all. They said. "We will show you the Xray pictures"—hoping to convince me that I was wrong. But I answered, "Xray pictures or no Xray pictures, that arm is not going to be amputated." However, they protested and argued that gangrene would set in— if it had not already done so. I said, "I will ask God Almighty to not let that happen." Then turning to the doctors, I said, "Shame on you doctors; if you cannot do it, I can, only I have no license. . . " And to Dr. Seversen I said, "Will you do it? Tell me quick, for if you will not, I will take him away from here." The doctor replied, "I will."

I said to Dr. Seversen, "I would like to go along with you to see whether you know how to do it." Eight doctors were also present. While the doctor was drilling a hole in the protruding bone, red blood spurted out of it, and I said, 'Praise the Lord!" One of the doctors standing by said, "How do you know that that looks good?" I made no reply, but looked at him with a grin.

During his stay in the hospital I visited the young man from time to time. One day I asked the doctor how he was getting along with Elder, and he answered, "Getting along good only the sore doesn't quit running as rapidly as I would like to have it." Then I ventured, "Have you looked at his back?" He asked, "Tuberculosis of the spine?" I replied, "You had better look."

The next time I was there he said, "There is no tuberculosis about him now; he is well, when did he have it?" Then I told him that five years previous to this time, when a lad of fourteen, he was sick and I prayed for him and the Lord healed him. (Dr. Seversen did a good job on that young man's arm and the Lord did the finishing.) Mr. Larson has a good strong arm today and is employed in a service station in Elbow Lake, Minnesota.

Two years later I visited Dr. Seversen. When he saw me, he stuck both arms up and said, "Here comes the man with the iron nerve." I answered him, "No, here comes the man with a little good common sense and faith in God Almighty." "Yes," he said, "common sense, but I thought it could not be done, when it was in such a mess and had been broken so long." I answered him, "Yes, but a good arm is better than an iron hook on it." He said, "Indeed, but I did not think it could be done." (I have nothing against doctors, but the Lord can do what men cannot do.)

─ : : : : ─

One time Brother and Sister George Larson's three sons were stricken at the same time with infantile paralysis. Herman was 21 and the twins 18 years. A specialist was called and he brought two doctors with him. He pronounced the cases as very serious, especially Norman who was stricken in the head, and they did not think there was any hope for him. They said it would be a good thing if he would die, for if he lived, he would be crazy. They sent for me. Sister Larson was then pastor of a congregation in Hereford, Minn. They had been praying and we prayed again, and the Lord finished the job and healed all three. Often people say, "It was not so serious and may not have been what they said it was," but this time the devil got fooled. The young man had been going to the University of Minnesota where they had been tapping some blood from them for medical science purposes to use to heal others stricken in the same manner; so medical science acknowledge they had the real thing.

At one of the camp meetings at Hereford, Ole Torgesen got very much under conviction and went home to repair a thrashing machine engine. It did not want to start and he got angry and swore at it. Starting suddenly the fly wheel struck his left hand and breaking a number of bones. He went to the doctor and had the bones set and the hand taped and the arm strapped to his body. Then he came back to the meeting and wanted to be saved. He repented, and the Lord accepted him. While he was still on his knees he looked up and said, "I hear you men believe in divine healing, and I want to be prayed for that the Lord will heal my hand." So Brother C. H. Tubbs and myself prayed the prayer of faith and he began to unloose his arm and take off the bandage. While he was doing so, the saints were shouting the praises of God. Others told him not to take the bandage off and got angry as he continued removing them. Finally he took off the cotton and cleaned off the iodine and the taping. After doing so, he lifted his arm slowly to move his fingers. Finally he put his hand up and moved his fingers freely, and his hand was healed to the glory of God. Next day we had baptismal services and I asked him if he wanted to be baptized. He said he did, but thought his wife would be saved, too, so wished that both could be baptized together. I said, "All right."

Next day in the morning service she got saved. She was the daughter of a lay minister of a certain denomination who did not believe in baptism by immersion. She asked me if they could be baptized right away. I told her that just as soon as the service was over we would go immediately to the pool. She did not want her parents to know what she was doing, so we kept it quiet, but when we started for the pool, the prairie seemed to be alive with people on horse back and in all kinds of rigs, coming from all directions.

They were blowing horns and making music on circle saws. So when we got to the pool, the banks were covered with people more than in the baptismal service before. While we were singing, I heard the sister say to her husband, "There they come!" It was her father and mother. They came over to them and I said, 'Don't say a word to them." The preacher went after them in a great way. Finally the daughter put her arms around his neck, and said, "Daddy, don't go at it this way, please. We are saved now and want to obey the commandments of the Lord." "All right," he said, "You are old enough to know what you are doing." "But this man . . . ," running at me and shaking his fist in my face, and I thought I surely would get a good licking when I said nothing and did not move. He cooled down, and said, "This is a poor man. We better take up a collection for him," and walked away. While I was baptizing the two and a Methodist minister's son, stones and sticks flew in plenty around me but none hit me.

One evening three young men cut the rope of the tent and were caught. When they learned they could get seven years in State prison, and we did not prosecute them—that ended all the disturbance at that place.

———— : : : : ————

At one time I was holding a revival meeting at Plum Coulee, Canada. One evening there was conviction upon a number of people. I was just going to close my sermon and make the altar call, and the devil said, "Now you swear." It shocked me so, I had to stop for a minute and conviction ceased. Then I had to start preaching again. The devil once more said, "Now you swear." I rebuked him and went ahead and made the altar call, and those under conviction came forward and received help.

MAN FEAR

I was called at one time to Grand Forks to help in a meeting. Coming there, I saw two or three large, tall ministers whom I had never seen before. I was scared to preach before them, so when we had prayer that evening, I prayed the Lord to deliver me from man fear. The committee asked me to speak that evening and the Lord blessed and gave me victory. Next day one of those good ministers came to me and said, "I want to talk to you. I was so blessed before you came, but since you came, I was afraid of you and my blessing all left. I wonder if you can help me?" "I can," I said. "When I came last night, upon seeing you and Brother H., I got so scared I wished I was not here, so I prayed and it left me and then the devil jumped on you."

This made me think of a Swedish song which says in part:
"Menisko frygtens didlige snaror har bringat
Mangen en man paafald."
Which means in English:
"The fear of man the deadly snares
Has brought many a man to fall."

In a case like this it may not mean so much, but in many cases good ministers have failed to preach the truth because of the fear of man. What a disaster for themselves and for hundreds of souls!

One Sunday morning I spoke in a chapel for a brother pastor. When the service was over he came to me and in a very tired tone, he said, "Did you mean me this morning?" I answered, "Dear Brother, I surely did not mean you." He said, "Well," and walked away still tired. I did not go for lunch but remained in the chapel and wept and prayed that I might not be a trial to my dear brethren. I said, "I will not go into the pulpit again until you give me more wisdom," but when the afternoon meeting time came, no one else had a message, and I had to go into the pulpit again. The Lord blessed in a wonderful way, and a number of souls got saved. After the service the good pastor came to me and said, "Will you forgive me? You did not mean me this morning."

———: : : :———

HOW THE LORD LEADS

Once on my way to Platte, South Dakota, I got lost. I was driving slowly trying to think of where I had gotten off my route—when suddenly a man in a field on a tractor waved me to stop. He climbed over the fence, and here it was Brother Walter Ratzlaf. He said, "How come you are here?" I answered, "I'm lost." "Turn around," he answered, "and we will drive down to the house."

Going to the house, there was a young lady I had known in North Dakota. He introduced her to me as his wife. The last time I had seen them, they were in North Dakota. Both of them were now members of the committee for the young people's convention of North Dakota, which was to convene the following Friday, Saturday and Sunday. George W. Green of Bertha, Minnesota was to have been the guest speaker, but they had just gotten a telegram from him saying that he could not be there. Brother Ratzlaf said, "The Lord must have sent you here. Could you be our guest speaker?" I answered, "Yes, if you want me. I am on my way home, and Brother Green was expecting to meet me at my place, and I was planning on taking him from my home on to the convention." Again, I could see how the Lord directed many times, unbeknowns to me.

A lady brought her sister who was in the last stages of tuberculosis to the camp meeting at Saint Paul Park, Minn. Wife and I prayed for the sick woman and she was instantly healed. So they insisted that I go to their place and hold them a meeting. I was very busy, so it was sometime before I could go. Finally they wrote asking how much I wanted to hold the meeting. I wrote that my carfare round trip was to be $26.50, and I thought I ought to have that much. They answered that they would give me that much, and that much more. I went and started the meeting on Friday evening. The folks I was to stay with lived six miles in the country and we secured the Methodist Church in town for the services. We had two services on Saturday, three on Sunday, two Monday and two Tuesday. Tuesday night they left me in the church. I had coal enough to keep me warm. As I had no money to go to the hotel, the next morning I walked out to their place in the loose snow, arriving about dinner time. I had dinner and that evening they took me to the meeting and left me again. I have no recollection of how I got away from there. It seems to me a family in town, who knew some of my relatives, kept me for a day or two. My carfare, which I still have coming from them as well as the rest, is the only meeting I had held in 52 years on which I had set a price. A brother belonging to another denomination who often attended the services and who was an agent for the Furges Kalls Woolen Mills, Minnesota, whom I met some years later, asked me, "Did you ever get any money from that meeting?" I replied, "I have it all coming," so he gave me five dollars and a pair of seven dollar trousers. That experience was one of the "all things." This was the only time I ever set any price on my ministry.

PRAYER CHANGES THINGS

Brother Masters and I were holding meeting in Hereford, Minnesota. Brother Masters was doing most of the preaching, and I was exhorting and giving the invitations. One evening after he finished preaching, I dismissed the meeting immediately. As we were going to our room between eleven and twelve, he asked, "Why did you not give the altar call tonight?" Then he added, "You did right, but what was the reason?" I answered, "Too much Masters." He replied, "The Lord help me!" and on his knees he went. He stayed there until between three and four o'clock in the morning. The next night I did not need to give an altar call, for the people flocked to the altar of their own accord.

MY FIRST PREACHING TRIP

I was standing in a wagon driving home from Hawick, Minnesota. The Lord spoke to me and said, "I want you to go to Belgrade next Sunday and preach." I replied, "I do not know what to preach." The Lord answered, "You go and open your mouth wide, and I will fill it." I argued that I did not have the money to go. He answered, "I'll tend to that."

When I arrived home from Hawick, there was a letter from an old brother about 80 years of age living at Norway Lake, Minn. He said, "The Lord has been telling me that you ought to go to Belgrade and hold them a meeting, and I am sending you the carfare." So I went.

Another time I was holding a meeting north of Belgrade and staying with Brother and Sister Andrew Larson. The night before leaving that locality I dreamed that when I came to Belgrade, I saw a man go into the depot just ahead of me, and as he stepped away from the ticket window he said, "Ha, ha, ha, I may as well go home then, since there is no train until three o'clock this afternoon."

Brother Larson was to take me to the depot early in the morning, and it was cold. When telling them my dream they laughed, and we all laughed. They said, "It can't be that bad."

It was about six miles to town and riding in an open buggy, I got cold, and when we got within about a quarter mile from town, I said, "You had better let me out here and I will walk and get warmed up." So he did. When I arrived at the depot a man walked in just ahead of me, and when he turned from the window, he said, "Ha, ha, ha, I might just as well go home since there will be no trains until three o'clock this afternoon."

I walked up to the ticket window and said, "How come the train is so late?" He said, "An old freight train ran off the track and they will have to clean up before the passenger train can come through." I did not wait, but walked home—a distance of twenty miles.

———— : : : : ————

At one time I held a meeting in what was known as Clark school house, fifteen miles south of Cohasset, Minnesota. After the last Sunday morning service, I said, "If there is anyone who will take me to Cohasset after service tonight, my heavenly Father will give him a hundred fold in this life, and eternal life in the world to come." So going down to the door after service to shake hands with the folks, there stood a nice looking young man who had not been out to the services before. He said, "I'll take you to town tonight." I said, "All right, thank you," and out he went. After a while Brother Goodell, the elder, came and said, "I'll take you to town." I said, "You are too late. You lost your pay this time." He said, "Who is going to take you?" I answered, "The young man who stood by the door when I got there." He thought a while, then he said, "Oh, that was Henry Garber; that will never do. He is not saved. He drinks a little, dances, plays cards and likely smokes. Then he added, "I'l take you. The road is bad" (and it surely was.) I answered him, "If he is like that he needs the pay." "Well," he said, "He may not come. Aren't you afraid to go with him?" "No," I said.

He came, and it took us quite a while to get there on account of the road. We talked farming, dancing, drinking, love and salvation. Getting to town, it was still an hour and a half before the train would arrive. He said, "Wouldn't it be good to have a little lunch now?" I said, "That would be fine." "Alright," he said, "you order what you want." "Aren't you going to have some?" I asked; but he said, "no." After lunch he said, "How about a little ice cream now." "Fine," I said.

There were quite a number of young folks in the restaurant and while I was eating he was talking to the young people telling them he had been to two services that day and he added, "They were two of the best sermons I have ever heard in my life." They called out in a chorus, "Henry, Henry, have you sworn off?" Then they asked, "Who preached?" He answered, "Reverend Susag over here."'

After I got through eating, he introduced me to all those young people. Then I said, "You had better get me to the depot now, and start for home; the road is so bad." "Well," he said, "I will not start back until you are on the train." And so he did; and when he put my grips on the train, he said, "Good by," and as he shook hands with me he left $3.00 in my hand. As he was leaving me he said,

"When—" but he never finished what he started to say. No doubt he meant to say, "When you pray remember me."

I did not hear of him, nor see him for two or three years. Going to Milwaukee one Sunday to hold services for Brother Flint, a young man came to me in the chapel and said, "Praise the Lord Brother Susag." I said, "Amen." I looked at him and he said, "Do you know me?" I answered, "Yes, I have met you somewhere, but I don't remember where." "Think of Cohasset, Minnesota," he answered. I slapped him on the shoulder and said, "Henry, when did you get saved?" "Driving home that night," he said; "thinking how you treated me, almost a stranger, you spoke to me like a father—with such good understanding of everything and you called me brother and I got broken up, and going to my room on the farm, I knelt by my bed and repented and the Lord saved me. It was so good and the Lord made me so happy. I went to see my parents who lived six miles out of Milwaukee, Wisconsin." They all became members of the congregation in Milwaukee, and Henry became a much loved and respected member of the congregation in Grand Rapids, Minnesota, and for many years one of the leaders and finally went home to his reward.

―― : : : : ――

One time I was holding a meeting in the neighborhood where a young man lived who was one of our first converts, and he attended my services. One day he asked me if I would go home with him. I said, "Yes." On the way, he stopped me and said, "Have you got grace enough?" I answered, I think so." Finally we got near his home, and in a little grove he stopped me again and he repeated, "Have you got grace enough?" I answered again, "I think so, but if you think I need more, let us pray that the Lord will give me all that I need." We knelt down in the grove there and prayed. Coming into the house he introduced me to his mother, a fine looking lady. We sat down and had a friendly chat, and before I knew it, I said, "Praise the Lord."

"Oh," she said, "You are one of them are you?" Then she gave me a real tongue lashing. This was because several of her sons and daughters had gotten saved, and they were very much persecuted because they left their church. Sometimes when she would find Olaf on his knees praying, she would grab him by the hair and pull him around in the house.

Finally her husband came in, and she introduced me to him.

"Susag," he said, "Are you the husband of that witch over near Paynesville or Hawick, that goes singing and finegring on the strings on that box, getting people to weep and taking them away from their parents?" (Wife played a harp when she sang.) Then he said, "You get out of this house as fast as your feet can carry you." I took my hat and started for the door, and as I came near, he stood there with his hatchet in his hand and said, "if you come nearer, I will smash your head," and lifted the hatchet, and then I realized the man was so angry he did not know what he did say. So I went back and sat down. "Say, Mr. Erickson," I said, "Sit down, and let me tell you how the Lord saved us." "Alright," he answered. His wife said, "Get him out, get him out!" Then he answered, let him speak out of his heart. It is the first time he has ever been in our house." "No," she said, "Get him out." "No, no, wife, be quiet." And he sat down and I related how the Lord convicted wife and I. (We used to be of the same faith as they were). When I had told them our experience, he came over and put his hand on my shoulder, and said, "You can stay with us over night, but don't say anything about your religion."

I thanked him and said, "We have services tonight, and I have to be going."

Later on Brother Peter Peterson of Foboken, New Jersey and myself held a meeting in that neighborhood and went and called on Mr. Erickson, and had a very pleasant visit with him. Brother Peterson had been a rough seaman and he told him of his life, and how the Lord had convicted and saved him. That seemed to impress him.

Years later Olaf bought the farm and his parents moved to another house. One morning Mr. Erickson did not come in for breakfast, and his wife went to his bedroom to see what was the matter. There he was on his knees by the bed praying. The first time she had ever seen him doing so in that position. He got up and said, "yes, I am coming." She went back to the kitchen, but still he did not come; so she went back to call him. Again he was on his knees by the bed. She said, "Aren't you coming husband. The breakfast is getting cold." He answered again, "Yes, I'm coming." But he did not come yet. She went back the third time, and on his knees he was, and this time he was dead. No doubt the man had been calling upon God, and the Bible says, "Whosoever calleth on the name of the Lord shall be saved." Hundreds of prayers had gone up for those folks. After his death Mrs. Erickson went to stay with her oldest daughter at Westlake, Minnesota. After being there for some time she took very sick, and she said to her daughter, "Will you send for the preacher?" Yes, she said, "What is his address?" (thinking she wanted her own pastor). "No," she said, "I want your pastor, Brother Susag." I went and at the end of three days, she got gloriously saved and got well. Later on she took sick again and passed on, and because I was in Europe at the time, my wife conducted the funeral service. What looks hopeless with man can be changed by prayer.

———: : : :———

At one time when Olae Christaphersen was selling books in the country between Grove City and Litchfield, Minn., he came to a home where quite a number were weeping and he asked why they were so sad. The lady of the house replied, "Our daughter, a young lady, is in the bedroom dying, and husband has gone to town to get the coffin, as she stinks already." (Those days they took the coffin to the homes sometimes). He inquired if he could see her, and she said, yes. After standing looking at her a while, he knelt and laid his hands on her and prayed the prayer of faith, and the Lord raised her up. Years later he was selling books in N. Dakota. He came to a nice farm home and knocking at the door a fine looking lady opened the door. Surprising him, she said, "Come in." Unused to such courtesy, he hesitated a moment, and she said again, "Come in, I know you. I am the lady you prayed for down by Litchfield, Minnesota, whose father had gone to the undertaker to arrange for the funeral. I am married and this is my home."

———: : : :———

At one time a sister-in-law of Olae Christaphersen, Bastine Christaphersen, was in childbirth. The midwife said the child could not be born without medical help. Her husband started for Wilmer to get the doctor. At seven o'clock she began to get blue and lost consciousness. They sent for Brother Olae. When he came, he looked at his sister-in-law and walked out into the woodshed, and there among the split wood he knelt down and prayed. A number of times they called for him to come in, but he did not answer. About twelve o'clock he came hurrying in and laid his hands on his sister-in-law and said, "I command in the name of the Lord Jesus Christ that this child be born, and that my sister-in-law be made well." Immediately the child was born, and all was well. In a few minutes the doctor arrived and he said it was a wonderful miracle.

HEALED AFTER RUNNING A RUSTY NAIL THROUGH THE FOOT

One time my wife stepped on a rusty nail, running it through the shoe sole and her foot. The next morning Brother Christaphersen came and she asked him to make her a crutch, since I was in Europe at the time. She had to walk with her knee on a chair and he said he would. He went out and in a few minutes he came back and said, "The Lord does not want me to make you a crutch. Let us pray the Lord to heal you." They prayed and she was healed at once.

HEALED OF LOCKJAW

I had my collar bone broken three times; the third time I was in North Dakota holding meetings. It was during July and very hot, being around 85 to 90 degrees in the shade. I was staying with Brother and Sister E. Olson and lockjaw set in. I took chills until they moved me into the kitchen and had the stove red hot. Even then I could hardly quit chilling. I battled with the devil and the pain for a whole day, and finally got the victory. Bless His name.

HEALED OF BROKEN LEG

One time I was plowing and was thrown off the seat onto the plow in such a way that my leg caught between the bars and I was thrown with my weight on my leg, breaking it near the ankle and splitting the bone nearly to the knee. The end of the broken bone protruded under the skin near the knee. The neighbor hearing my scream, phoned to my home, and the folks came and took me home. We sent for Sister Hendricks, (now Sister Mayhre). She and wife prayed for me and as they prayed the bone moved back into its place and the next day I was well as ever and able to go about my business.

MAN SAVED AND HEALED

At one time while I was pastor in Grand Forks, a young man came who had been on crutches for four years. (He was partially paralyzed, and unable to bear his weight on his limbs). He came at the time of the State camp meeting). He had written to Brother E. E. Byrum to come and pray for him, and he was bringing the answer he had gotten from Brother Byrum which said, "I haven't time to come and furthermore it is so far and expenses would be so great and since the Dakota State Camp meeting convenes in a few days, you might be able to get someone to take you down there. Brother Susag will be there and he does the same kind of work that I do. He will pray with you, and instruct you how to get saved and healed."

He came and went through the entire camp meeting without receiving the faith he needed to get saved and healed, but he remained another day and I had time to more thoroughly instruct him. He did get saved and was perfectly healed.

A DOCTOR'S DAUGHTER HEALED

I was asked at one time to come to a certain city to preach for a certain denomination for a couple of weeks, which I did. On coming I found that I was to stay with a certain doctor who had a daughter five years old. One afternoon she was sitting talking with me and I found her almost as smart as a high school girl. Toward evening I said to her, "Honey, you are sick." She shrugged her shoulders and said, "I'll be all right in the morning." But she became seriously ill that evening, insomuch that the next day her father sent for another doctor, a nurse and a lady to help. About three o'clock the third morning the doctor came up into my room and made a confession which he needed not to have made. Then he said, "I've come to my wit's end; I know of no help for the child. But would you please pray for her? But pray right away, as she may pass away any time." I began to pray right away. I put on my clothes and ran down stairs, praying all the while. When I got down stairs everything was quiet, and when the doctor met me, he said, "Less than three minutes after you commenced to pray my daughter went to sleep, and I believe when she wakes up she will be well." She slept until four in the afternoon. When she awakened, she said, "I want to get up and dress." The doctor said, "No, honey, you can't do that; you have been awful sick. You will have to stay in bed and be quiet until you get stronger." She said, "Where is Brother Susag?" He said, "Do you want to see him?" She said, yes, so they called me and I said, "Praise the Lord, honey." She said, "Can't I dress?" "Sure, you can dress," I said, and so they dressed her. Then she said, "Now I want to get up and run." Again the doctor said, "You can't do that." She said, "Brother Susag, can't

I run?" I said, "Sure, you can run," and out of the bed she went, but she stumbled against the wall, and the doctor went to catch her. She said, "Don't touch me. If I need help, Brother Susag can help me." Then through the house she ran with the father, mother and nurse after her. I was standing in the middle of the room praising God. Finally she stopped and faced her father and said, "Can't I run, daddy?" He said, "Sure you can, honey."

Her father came and put his arms around my neck weeping and said, "You saved the life of my child." I answered, "No, I didn't." He said, "Who did then?" I said, "You made a humble confession and asked one of the Lord's servants to pray, and the Lord honored your faith and healed her." "Yes," he said, "but if you hadn't been here she would have been dead now."

A humble confession is a sure stepping stone to faith.

HEALED OF PARALYSIS

Not long ago the Lord said to me. "You go to such and such a church tonight," which I did. After service was over, a man who had been paralyzed from his waist down for a long time, asked me to pray for him. The prayer of faith was offered and he was instantly healed. To corroborate the above, will say that later I met a minister of another denomination who knew the case and he said that this man had retained his healing.

DELIVERED FROM A SINKING SHIP

I wish to rewrite an incident given in Brother E. E. Byrum's book, "Startling Incidents and Experiences in the Christian Life." As it was given to him verbally, and I did not see the manuscript to correct it after it was written. But on reading the article in his book, I discovered that he had forgotten some of the facts. I am rewriting it here, praying that it may prove a blessing.

For the glory of God I desire to relate some incidents connected with my trips to Scandinavia in the years 1904-05. While I was engaged in evangelistic work in North Dakota in the fall of 1904, the brethren in New York City wrote me about making them a visit. After praying earnestly for the Lord to make known his will in the matter, I decided to go, and felt that if I went to New York I also ought to make a trip across the Atlantic to Norway to see my parents and relatives whom I had not seen for twenty-four years.

In the latter part of November it was made very clear to me by the Holy Spirit that I should go, and about the middle of December I left my home for New York City. On the 24th of December my wife took so seriously ill that she was not expected to live. She had faith that the Lord would raise her up, but the children were much distressed, fearing that their mother was going to die, and knowing that their father was on his way to a foreign land, not intending to return for several months. They begged to have a telegram sent to me asking me to return. Finally about two o'clock in the night, when she was getting very low, and the children would not be comforted in any other way, she consented to have a telegram sent to the missionary home in New York City. Knowing as she did that it was God's will for me to go to Norway and knowing also that if I returned so soon, I could not go if she should recover, she prayed earnestly that the Lord would hinder me from getting the telegram, which he did. God heard her prayer and also healed her. After stopping with the church in New York for sometime, I went to Boston, and thence on the 20th of January, 1905 sailed on the Steamship Saxonia of the Cunard line for Liverpool, Eng. Everything went well—the Atlantic was the smoothest I had ever seen it. I wondered how it could be otherwise, inasmuch as my family and many people of God were sending up earnest prayers for my safe journey. My journey from Liverpool to Hull was by railroad, but at the latter place, I embarked on the S. S. Tasso of the Wilson Line bound for Tronheim, Norway. Getting into the North Sea we had a very rough voyage. We were to make our first stop at Stavanger, but the weather was so stormy as we neared the coast that evening that we did not dare to sail in the dark. Consequently we anchored out in the North Sea for the night. While the ship tossed up and down and back and forth through the night, I dreamed the ship was going on dry land. I could hear the screeching as it went on the rocks and chills went down my back. Then the scene changed. In my dream I seemed to be on land standing looking at the ship going, and wondering why it did not tip over. I looked close and on the right hand side of the ship was a large stone, almost as high as the ship, scraping against its side. On the left side was a small stone steadying it as it moved along. Finally it moved out into deep water and turned to the left, and in a little while we landed at our destination, Tronheim. In the morning I told my dream at the breakfast table and said, "We may have an accident before we get through. The people laughed and said, "Do preachers believe in dreams?" I said, "Yes, when they come true." They thought there was no danger, for the reason the ship was so large. "Well," I said, "it is very stormy weather and the sea is full of rocks along the coast and we do not know what may happen." That day we landed safely in Stavanger, and then went to our next stop, Bergen. Leaving there we encountered the roughest sailing I had ever experienced. Four ships started out at the same time from the dock, and only one was able to anchor at the next stop, Aalesund, so we had to anchor out in the ocean. The next morning we were able to land at the dock. Thence we went to Christiansund, which was our last stop before our final destination. It was a good harbor, and were ready to leave there at 8 p.m., but as the storm was still raging out in the sea, the captain decided to remain in the harbor until twelve o'clock. Then we should land at our destination at eight o'clock in the morning. At twelve o'clock we left the harbor. The storm was still raging and a heavy snow was falling. At 1:15 a.m. I felt a shock and heard the same screeching noise that I had heard in my dream and knew at once what had happened. Immediately the stewart came running into the stateroom calling, "Everybody up! take nothing along. We are sinking!"

Quicker than I can tell you the seven men with me in the stateroom were up and dressing, putting on all the clothes they could. Up the stairs they went, throwing away their tobacco and pipes, and leaving behind their whisky bottles, some empty and some partly empty. I got up, dressed, took my Bible and read a little. Then I knelt down and had prayer. The stewart came down and said, "Aren't you in a hurry? We are sinking!" I said, "No, he that believeth shall make no haste." He looked at me and went on the deck. The snow storm was whistling wildly through the tackling of the ship, and the seamen were working with all their might to lower the life boats. Others were running to and fro. Some women were crying aloud and others were praying while the water was pouring into the sides of the ship. The pumps were working to their full capacity, throwing out the water. It was indeed a sad sight. As a seaman was running by, I asked him to direct me to the pilot. He looked at me and said in a harsh voice, "What do you want with the pilot?" and went his way. A little further on I met another seaman, and asked him the same question. He said, "The pilots are both over there with the captain," pointing to three men who were standing a short distance away.

I walked over to where they were standing, conversing with one another. I saluted them and said to the captain. "Could you spare me a minute or two?" "If it is important, I can," he replied. "I think it is," I said. "Speak on then," he said. I then asked him who the pilot of the boat was, and one pointed to himself and another man. Then I said to the head pilot, "We are off the rock now, are we not?" "Yes," he answered. "Did you turn to the left when you turned off the rock," I asked. "Yes," he replied. "If that is the case we need not go into the life boats," I replied, "as this boat is going to land in Tronhein, without loss of life." The captain looked at me and said, "What do YOU know about navigation, man?" pointing to the water that was being pumped out of the ship. "We are sinking." "I know nothing about navigation," I replied. "Explain yourself," he said. Then I told my dream and when I had finished speaking, I saw the tears running down the weather-beaten cheeks of the pilots. Then the captain said, "What kind of a man are you?" I answered, "An ordinary minister." Then the pilot said to the captain, "We had better listen to this man. He may be more right than we because as long as this ship can hold up we are safe, but if we go into the boats in this fearful weather and dark night, we shall soon be dashed to pieces against the rocks." Then the pilot said to me, "Our ship sticks 28 feet in the water and the rock we struck was only twelve feet under the water, so you see it is a great miracle that our ship is not in two, and one end on each side of the rock. Had that happened, no one would have known what became of us, for we are now in 53 fathoms of water." Orders were then given not to lower the life boats. (Then I said to the captain, "Is this the Tasso, that used to sail on Norway 24 years ago?" He replied, "No, that lays on the bottom of the sea six miles from here." Then he said, "What about it?" I said, "I embarked on that ship at Tronheim the 27th day of April on a Sunday afternoon at four o'clock of the year 1881 with 384 other young people who were sailing for England on our way to America. At nine o'clock we got into an awful snowstorm and just lay drifting until one fifteen, A. M. exactly the same time of night as we struck the rock this time. We went on the rock and turned over on the side just outside of the Agness lighthouse. Then the captain said, "What kind of a man are you?" "Just an ordinary minister," I answered. The captain then told me his father was captain of that ship at that time." It might be interesting to the reader to know that we lay on our side until almost six fifteen in the morning when the ship straightened up as the tide arose. Then they cut the anchor chain and we backed up and went our way). Needless to say, that night was one of the greatest prayer meetings ever held.

While I was speaking with the Captain, the first mate had come, a fine tall Englishman. "Will you kindly go with me to the front end of the ship and see if we can see any lights? We are lost. We don't know where we are." I answered, "I know nothing about navigation sir." He said, "Please go with me." I did, and coming out there, I saw three lights, and he could not see any. He said, "Keep your eyes on them, and I'll run for the captain." They both came running and the captain could not see the lights either. Turning to me he said, "You must be mistaken." "No sir,"

I replied, "I can see them now." He then asked me the color of the lights. After I had given him a description of them, he saw them himself and explained, "They are steamers. Where are we? We are lost!" He called out in agony.

We lay there until six fifteen in the morning. When we turned around to the right between the rocks, they knew where to go. The pumps were in full operation, but our ship was tipping backward more and more as if it were going to stand on one end. We landed in Tronheim in the afternoon with our handsatchels and our lives, and as soon as the pumps stopped, the ship filled with water and sank in the harbor.

I saw an account of the wreck in two Norwegian papers after the ship had been raised and placed on dry dock. The paper stated that the cargo was a total loss and the ship was about thirty eight thousand dollars. That nearly every plate from midship to stern was torn loose, just as I had seen in my dream and the paper said they could not understand why the ship had not sunk before, as one plate hole was enough to sink the ship. My wife wrote me later and said, "I know why the ship did not sink. I and many others were praying that God would keep that ship on top of the waves, because he had one of his little ones on the ship." The Lord verified his promises by hearing the prayers of his people to protect me and bring me safely to my destination. The blessings of salvation never seemed more real to me than at that time, as I was enabled to be calm and quiet through all the perils, having the sweet assurance that the mighty arm of God was upholding me and protecting not only me, but those who were traveling with me. He hears and answers prayers. Those who trust and believe in him he often saves from death and destruction.

HOMEWARD BOUND

My return trip was just as eventful as my trip to Norway. For some time I had been praying earnestly for the Lord to direct me in getting the right ship across the ocean, as I was to sail during the stormy season of Spring. On the twentieth of March, 1905, I left the home of my parents in Norway, with the intention of sailing the next morning. I was to sail on an English boat bound for Hull, England, in order to reach the fastest boat on the Cunard Line bound from Liverpool to New York, as I thought that would be the best vessel to take. Soon after leaving my fathers home, I stopped at a little seaport called Levanger to visit a relative of mine for a few hours, expecting to leave on the evening train, but my relative persuaded me to stay and take the early morning train. He said I would have ample time to reach my boat in Tronhiem, but when my train entered the station the next morning, the ship upon which I had intended sailing was just leaving the harbor.

I did not understand what this meant, but remembered the scripture which said that "All things work together for good to those that love the Lord." Had my plans for reaching the fast steamer from Liverpool to New York carried and had the ship sailed on schedule, I should have been in New York in ten days, but now I had to make the best of the situation, so I decided to embark on the S. S. United States of the Scandinavian American Line from Oslo which was due in New York just one week later than the other ship, and if run on schedule generally arrived in New York nine days after leaving Oslo.

We sailed from Oslo on time, but after being out at sea for a day, we found to our surprise and dissatisfaction of many of the passengers that instead of going direct to

New York, we had to go to the Azores to pick up some passengers from another ship of the same line, as a shaft of that ship had been broken in a storm on the Atlantic Ocean, and the ship had been towed to some Island. This made a very long round-about voyage.

With the exception of two or three days of storm, the weather was good, but the waves rolled exceedingly high every day. By this we knew that farther north in the ocean, a terrible storm was raging.

Finally after fifteen days of rough sailing, we found ourselves just outside New York in the midst of a heavy fog, such as I had never before witnessed. The whistles of the fog horns of the ships kept blowing and the bells ringing as we slowly proceeded in the afternoon, but finally we had to anchor, as a pilot from the shore entered our ship and forbade us to go any further. He said the sea was full of anchored ships on account of the fog, some of which had been there for three days. He said we could not move until the wind changed and drove the fog away. I felt quite satisfied, although like many others, I had been very seasick while on the voyage. Early the next morning I went on the deck. There was so much unrest and grumbling among the passengers that it was quite unpleasant for me to stay on the ship any longer. However, the fog seemed to be thicker than ever. It was so dense a person could hardly see beyond his outstretched arm. I went to my room, and there while lying across the bed, prayed earnestly to God to take away the fog. Then I went on deck and looked, but the fog seemed to be still worse. I went down and prayed the second time, but found on my return the fog seemed to be thicker than ever. The third time I went and prayed, and while I was praying a voice said to me, "Change your clothes." I knew what it meant. The Lord had heard my prayers. I arose and put on my best suit of clothes (for I expected soon to be in New York). Then I went to the breakfast table.

The people were complaining on account of having to remain so long on the ship. I said, "Before we have finished breakfast, we shall be on our way into the harbor." Some asked who had said so. I said I had been praying to God and He had assured me that such would be the case. Eight men got up and laughed me to scorn, saying, "ha, ha, ha," but while we were eating we heard something rattle and someone asked. "What is that?" I said, "I suppose they are raising the anchor." A number sprang from their seats and looked through the portholes and the fog was gone, and we were on our way to the port. Then one man arose and said, "That minister's religion must be right." After that there was no more laughing and scorning. Thank God, he stood by me and showed himself mighty in answering my prayers and in lifting the fog to the astonishment of my fellow travelers. Our ship was the first one to pass into port, though some had been waiting there for three days for an opportunity to reach New York.

After landing, I learned that the Cunard liner on which I had intended to sail from Liverpool, had not yet arrived. It did not arrive until the next day. According to reports it had the worst voyage that any ship of that company had had for forty six years, and a number of passengers were badly hurt, being thrown about by the rolling and tossing of the ship. A young man who came across the ocean on that ship informed me that a number had to be tied to their beds, and many were injured. After learning these things, I perceived that the Lord had answered prayer in a wonderful way. He had hindered me from embarking on that ship, and had thus spared me much unnecessary suffering.

Thanks be to his precious and matchless name. It is safe to put our whole trust in God, because He knows how to protect and shield us from harm and danger. It is my prayer that the relating of this incident of the Lord's dealings with me may prove a blessing and inspiration to others, and enable them to put their whole trust in the Lord in time of difficulty and distress. He will surely hear and answer prayer when we call upon Him in a simple childlike manner.

AN ANSWER TO PRAYER

For the glory of God, I wish to relate two very definite instances of answered prayer.

One time I was holding services nine miles north of Kerkhoven, Minn. The meetings were very good, but I was under a very severe trial, and it seemed very difficult for me to learn the will of the Lord as to whether at the close of the meeting I should go home or to Grand Forks, North Dakota, Camp Meeting. I learned that my fare from Kerkhoven to Grand Forks would be $3.32. Then I went out into the grove three times, (I believe it was on Friday,) and asked the Lord that on Sunday forenoon at the close of the services He would put it in the mind of somebody to give me exactly $3.32 if He wanted me to go to Grand Forks. No one but the Lord knew my needs. On Sunday after the service while I was shaking hands with the people, a brother put some money in my outside coat pocket. When I left the house, I walked to the grove to the same spot where I had prayed and knelt down and thanked the Lord for $3.32 in my pocket, and when I had counted the money I found that it was the exact amount for which I had prayed. He had not only supplied my carfare, but had in this way made known His will to me. Before I left the next morning, the brethren had given me more, so that I had something to send to my family.

THE SECOND INCIDENT

The second incident I desire to relate, occurred at the time when the Lord made it very clear to me to go to a certain place in South Dakota to hold a meeting in a new place. This also was on Friday and I knew that the Lord was directing me to go on the following Wednesday. I was in need of a suit of clothes, as what I had was not fit to wear in public. I was also in need of carfare. An elderly sister was staying with us and together with my wife we had prayer and agreed that the Lord would supply these needs before Wednesday morning. While we were in prayer the Lord made it clear and definite that He would grant our petition. As we arose from our knees, I said, "Thank God, I have the money by faith." The elderly sister said, "Well, I suppose you will have to write to some of the well-to-do brethren and tell them your need." "No," I answered, "The Lord will tell them. I might make a mistake if I undertake to write to any of them." "You will not have the money then," she said. "Yes, mother," I said, "You will see before next Wednesday morning that I will have all I need." She doubted and said she would see.

The following Sunday we went to Colfax, Minnesota and held a service and received one dollar, and I said, "Thank God for one dollar." Then on Monday, I received a letter from a brother who lived near Sisseton, South Dakota which contained a check for seven dollars. The check was from a man whom I did not know that I had ever seen, and he did not know my address, but drove fifteen miles with a team and in a lumber wagon to another brother who knew my address. He told him to send it to me immediately, as he was impressed that I was in need. The old mother knew this brother and said he was well-to-do, and could well afford to send it. I said to her, "Did I not tell you that the Lord knew to whom to speak." She was very much astonished. I also received another letter in which there was a check from a brother whom I had not seen for four years. He wrote that while he was coming from Crookston, Minnesota to where he had been working, and was nearing Wadena, Minnesota, the Spirit of the Lord told him to hurry to the bank before it closed and send Brother Susag five dollars. In his letter he said he thought I must be in great need and that he hurried and reached the bank in time to get the money. He further said, "May the Lord bless you and use you to His glory."

Wednesday morning I started for Saint Paul, Minnesota with thirteen dollars in my pocket. Arriving there, I was looking for a second hand clothing store. I stood on the street praying for the Lord to direct me and He said, "Samuelson, Samuelson." I walked around a few blocks and suddenly I looked up over a store and it said, "Samuelson Second Hand Clothing." Going in, the merchant asked if he could help me. I said, "Have you a Prince Albert coat and vest that will fit me." He looked and said, "Just your fit," and walked over to a show case and brought the coat and vest and put it on me. It fit like it was made to order by a tailor. You could not see that it had even been on a man before. He said it was an eighty five dollar coat and vest, and it surely looked like it. It had silk facing on the lapels. I took off the coat, and put my own back on. I felt that I did not dare ask him the price. He said, "Aren't you going to take it." He took my coat off and put the coat back on me. Then I prayed the Lord for courage to ask him the price, so I said "What's your price?" He said, "A dollar and a half." I caught my breath and said, "What did you say?" He repeated, "A dollar and a half." I said, "Have you a pair of new trousers that will fit me?" I had to have the silk facing taken off, for fear I would be asked to the altar for too fine a suit.

I not only bought the coat and vest, but one new and one second hand trousers, and all came to $4.50.

Going to Arlington, I was dressed in the finest suit I had ever had in my life. I overheard two ladies speaking about me. One said, "You can see that man has seen better days by the fine clothes he wears." I wore that coat and vest for many years, and couldn't wear it out. Finally I got too stout and then I gave it away.

———: : : :———

At one time the Missionary Board was writing of the need in the Scandinavian countries, and wanted me to go immediately, though they were unable to finance me. Also the leading brethren of the Scandinavian Publishing Company at St. Paul Park almost demanded me to go. I prayed and wept, and said to the Lord, "Haven't you got any one else to go as you know I am a poor man, in debt on my home, and would be leaving my family in need, shifting for themselves." For three days it got darker and darker for me. Finally the third day toward evening I got desperate, and going into my bedroom, I prayed earnestly, not knowing where a penny of carfare would come from. As I was praying I said, "Listen, Lord, you know I am honest and earnest. Do not let me be deceived. I'll take one of these Bibles on the table, and close my eyes and throw it up in the air and catch it and the scripture my thumb is on when I catch it, I'll accept as an answer from you." I did so, and my thumb was on Mark 10:29-30. "And Jesus answered and said, 'Verily I say unto you, there is no man that hath left house or brethren or sisters or fathers or mothers or wife or children or lands, for my sake and the gospels, but he shall receive an hundred fold now in this time, houses and brethren and sisters and mothers and children and lands with persecutions, and in the world to come, eternal life.'" I said, "Amen." Then I got a phone message from Saint Paul Park saying, "We have been looking for you. Why don't you come?" My answer was, "I have no money." They said they had a check for thirteen dollars for me. I answered, "I am coming."

From there I went to Chicago to meet Brother E. E. Byrum who was president of the Missionary Board. He took me into a room and said, "It is almost cruel to demand you to go when we have no way to finance you, but the need is so urgent, and we know you have faith and the only thing I can do is to lay my hands on you and pray for you." He did so, praying and weeping, and when we got through he took out his purse and emptied it into my hand. It contained 94 cents. How I got there, I do not know.

I spent some time in Norway and Sweden visiting the churches holding revival meetings. From there I went on to Denmark where I spent thirteen months helping the dear faithful workers in raising up eight new congregations, making a total of thirteen. In 1916 the Missionary Board sent $25 per month for seven and one half months to wife and the children.

Before leaving Denmark, I visited all thirteen of the congregations which were there at that time, and preached my farewell sermon. In each place they gave me an offering and a large size envelope, thick and fat and written on the outside, "Not to be opened until on the North Sea or the Atlantic." When I opened them, there were many letters from different persons in each congregation expressing their appreciation for the help and blessing I had been to them. If I am not mistaken, there were 153 in all, and there was sufficient money in those letters to almost pay for my first car, a Ford. The promise previously quoted in Mark 10:29-30 was verily fulfilled.

———:::: ———

Once I was in great need of at least one hundred dollars and I had calls for three meetings at the same date. From one of these, I knew I would receive a hundred and twenty five dollars, and another, one hundred, but I knew the third could not give more than fifty. For three days I stayed home and prayed, and the Lord said I should go to the third, which I did.

On arriving at the place, I found they were closing a union meeting in one of the large churches the following day. They told me that the evangelist required them to forward him $500 before he would start his meeting, also $300 at the close of his meeting and $200 for his singer.

Monday night I began our service in the Church of God. One got saved. Tuesday night the crowd could not all get in the church. The Presbyterian minister of the town was there and he said it was too bad the people could not get in and offered us the Presbyterian Church free of charge. It was the largest church in town. We accepted and announced our meetings to be held there for Wednesday night. The church was packed and overflowing. Many were outside who could not get in. A 32nd degree Mason came to me and said, "Have you ever preached in a Masonic Hall?" I said I had preached in the Masonic Temple in Chicago, so he offered to get the Masonic Hall for me. I thanked him and accepted his offer, so the balance of the meeting was held there. It was filled for every service.

When the two weeks meeting was over, the church gave me $52.50 and the next day I was asked to come to a chain store; the manager said the store always gave a present to every evangelist who came to town. Then he said, "There is a present for you. What do you need? My wife says you need a pair of shoes, so go over to the counter and pick out a pair. They are fourteen dollars a pair." Then he said, "Come and sit down. I want to talk to you." Reaching his hand in his pocket he handed me a five dollar bill and said, "That's from me." Then the man who let me use the Masonic Hall came in. He said to the merchant, "Are you trying to persuade Mr. Susag to go with you to Norway to fish?" The merchant answered, "I wish I could." "So do I," he answered. Then he continued, "Mr. M., you know that you and I are about as low down in the mud as we can get, and every evangelist that comes to town is digging the hole deeper; but this man has kept on for two weeks doing his best to dig us out." The merchant answered, "That is right." Then the Mason handed me a check for ten dollars, and turning he said, "When—" and he walked away with tears in his eyes. Later on I understand he got saved and went to glory.

As I left the station that day for my home, many people came to the station to see me off and shook hands with me, leaving money in my hand or slipping it into my pockets. After I got on the train, I counted the money and found I had $187.00 instead of the fifty I had expected. Again God proved Himself to be the God that He says He is and His promises are true.

———— : : : : ————

TRIP TO EUROPE IN 1939

The Lord made it very clear to me that I should go to Europe again. I expected to stay four years. When it was understood that I was to sail for Europe, a number of people in a certain congregation requested me to stop over as they wanted to send greetings, so I did, thinking also that they might give me a little offering to help me on the way, but for some reason they failed to do so. The war broke out in Europe. I was able only to visit the churches, and late in the fall of the same year I was ordered to leave these countries. After being home for sometime, I met the wife of a minister and she asked, "Where have you been, Bro. Susag? We haven't seen you nor heard of you for so long." I told her I had been to Europe. "Why no," she explained, you were in such and such a congregation," (naming a place where I had stopped to receive greetings to carry to Europe). Then she said, "They said that you had not gotten any further than New York, as you did not have the money to go any farther." Then I told her, "The Lord made it very clear to me to go, so I went." After leaving this place for New York I was sitting on the train reading my Bible when a train man came along and said, "Are you reading the good book?" After answering yes, he asked if I was a minister. I answered "yes," and he asked where I was going. I told him I was on my way to Europe. "Do you have the finances supplied?" he asked. I told him I traveled by faith. "To what church do you belong?" he asked. I told him, the Church of God. So he explained, "My pastor is Brother—; What is your name?" When I told him, he said, "Why, I have heard of you." As he left he said, "Pardon me, I will see you again before we come to our divisional point." Later on he came and handed me a sum of money, so my needs were nicely cared for. On hearing of my experience, the sister exclaimed, "Why! God's promise, 'My God shall supply all your needs,' was fulfilled at that time."

ARRESTED FOR BEING A GERMAN DOCTOR

In 1915 I was on the Atlantic ocean on my way to Europe, and the captain came to me a number of times on the voyage, saying, "I am afraid you are going to have trouble if an English boat catches us before we get to Norway, because you claim to be a Norwegian by birth and a minister. We think you are a German by birth and a doctor. We had one sailing with us the last trip from Saint Paul, Minnesota and he spelled his name 'Susage' and was a German and a doctor. You spell your name 'Susag.' He had a goatee like you and looked just like you, and we think you two are brothers. We believe you are an American citizen, and if you acknowledge that you are a German and a doctor, we believe we can be a help to you. We will guarantee to the English people that we will take care of you and take you back to America the next trip."

I thanked him and smiled and said, "But I am still a Norwegian and a preacher, and I believe I am going to stand the test."

Sure enough a number of us were apprehended by an English war ship, and they sailed us into Kirkwall, Scotland and put nine of us (me included) under arrest. The fourth day a high official came from London to examine our papers, and I was the first one to march in between two rows of soldiers with bayonets on the guns ready for action. The captain and first mate were present to see how I was coming out. Finally a soldier called, "Halt!" and I assure you, I stopped and smiled at them all. I saluted the officer and handed him my papers After he had examined them thoroughly, he said to me, "Where were you born, Reverend?" I said, "in Norway." "What City?" "Stienkjer," I answered. "Will you tell us that in your own tongue?"

I did so; then he folded my papers nicely and handed them back to me, smiled and saluted and said, "Pass on; you are ok." I enjoyed the experience very much.

THE LORD GETS ME A CLERGY PERMIT ON THE RAILROAD

When the Lord saved me, he called me into the ministry. I knew the ministry were securing half fare on railroads, but did not know that they had to be ordained before they could get it. But I did know that the Lord had ordained me for the Ministry. So I went to the depot agent in my home town, and asked him if he would sign for me so I could have the benefits of clergy rates. He had known me for some years, so told me he could if I would swear that I was a preacher. I said, "No, I can't swear. If you can't take my word for it, I'll go without a permit." He said, "If you can't swear, I will sign for you." So I sent in my application to the clergy bureau, and a few days later I received the permit, but there was a little slip with it which said, "Are you wholly engaged in gospel work, or do you do some secular work?" I studied and prayed about it and wrote the clergy bureau and sent the permit back and said, "When I travel, I do nothing but gospel work, but when I am home, I preach twice on Sunday and once a week, and through the week I do whatsoever my hands find to do. I do not want any railroad bill against me in the day of judgment. So if you find upon this explanation that I am worthy of your courtesy, I will be very pleased to receive the permit, and if not, I thank you."

A few days later, the permit was returned to me with a letter saying, "Please accept our courtesy. We are not afraid of being imposed upon by a man like that."

When I was ordained, the brethren said, "Now you can get half fare on the railroads." "Well," I said, "I have had that almost seven years already." When I explained to them they were astonished.

A WONDERFUL EXPERIENCE

I was the evangelist at the South Dakota State Camp Meeting one year. After the meeting was over and I had received my offering from the committee, a brother came to me and wanted to give me $50 extra but I refused to accept it. "Why," he said, "Don't you need it?" "Yes," I said, "I need it badly, but I do not feel I can take it." "Well," he said, finally after much persuasion, "If you won't take it, I'll put it in the bank. For the Lord told me to give it to you, and I don't want it, and it will be there until you call for it."

About nine months later, I needed money and wrote him to see if I could borrow it until the next camp meeting. He sent it right away and wrote saying, "Thank God, it is out of my hands, and I'll never take it back again." At the next camp meeting, I tried again to pay it back, but I failed, so I went to prayer and asked the Lord what I should do. The Lord said, "You give Brother Renbeck fifteen dollars for a new suit, and you keep the rest for your family." (In those days one could get a good suit for fifteen dollars).

I looked for Brother Renbeck and finally he came. He had been weeping, although he still seemed happy. "Why have you been weeping?" I asked. "I need a new suit, and I went out and prayed and the Lord told me I could get a new fifteen dollar one." I reached my hand out and said, "Here is your fifteen dollars." He stepped back and said, "No, no! I couldn't take it from you. You need it worse than I do." I explained to him how it was, and he accepted it and praised the Lord. In those days we didn't know any different than to trust the Lord.

AN EXPERIENCE WITH TWELVE MINISTERS ON THE TRAIN

At one time while on the train in North Dakota, I sat down in the company of twelve ministers, representing that many denominations. While listening to them I decided that this was the time for a little fellow to keep his mouth shut. One young minister appeared to be the leader in the discussion standing with his Greek Testament in his hand. Finally he turned to me and said, "Are you a minister too?" I told him I was. "What denomination do you belong to?" I told him Church of God. "Well," he said, "If you belong to the Church of God, you have a horn in our side." I had met three of them once and they surely horned me. I said, "Yes, I've got a horn and I pity the minister that hasn't got one." (The horn represents power in scripture). "But," I said, "I use that on only one preacher." "Who is that," he said. "The devil." "Well," he said, "If you have one you have not showed it to us because you have kept still." Then turning, he pointed to each of the ministers individually asking each one what visible church of God he belonged to, and each answered, naming their own denomination. Then he said, "I belong to the visible Church of God Congregational." I spoke up then and said, "I belong to the visible Church of God." Then he slapped his hand on the arm of the seat and said, "You've got me, Brother." Then I said, "You see me, don't you?" "Yes," he said. "I see you, shake hands." Then he asked me how far I was going, saying that he would like to have a talk with me.

I told him I was going to Bismark, to which he said, "It is too bad that I change at the next station."

That ended the conversation. They seemed to have no more to say.

EXPERIENCE WITH TWELVE OTHER PREACHERS

When I was holding a meeting in a certain state, some of the church said there had been a couple of preachers holding services across the street from the Church of God chapel, and some of the saints had attended their meetings and became confused. They wanted me to preach against it. I said, "I cannot do that. The Word of God says, 'Thou shalt not judge a strange servant.' But I will pray the Lord to help me to meet them to get acquainted with their teaching." I did pray earnestly that I might meet them. Later I came to a town where I had to stay all night. I found twelve preachers there who were trying to start a new spiritual mushroom or work, and of the twelve preachers, two of them were the association preachers who had been holding the meetings across from our chapel in the town previously spoken of. I went to their service that evening and sat and prayed earnestly that if God was displeased with this new work they were trying to start, that the minister who was going to speak that night would have the hardest time preaching that he ever had in his life.

A minister arose to preach. His preaching was Biblical, but he had a hard time, while the other ministers kept on praying, "Lord, give the brother the anointing." He worked and perspired until all of a sudden he sat down. The ministers huddled together and talked and prayed and finally sent one of their number out into the audience to talk with the people. He finally wound up at me. He asked me a number of questions, whether I was saved and sanctified, and then left. But the ministers seemed to be dissatisfied, and sent another minister to me to investigate. At last he said, "I suppose the sermon tonight scared you." I said, "No, that was a good sermon and I have been preaching that way for over thirty eight years. That is the way the apostles preached."

"Well," he said, "We didn't know there was anyone preaching like that." Then I said, "But he had a hard time." "Yes," he answered, "He said he had the hardest time he had ever had in his life, and he has preached from the Atlantic to the Pacific and from Canada to the Gulf of Mexico and had never met anything like that he said." "Yes, and he was preaching against me." He replied, "Yes, and it was you that made it hard for him." Then I said, "I prayed earnestly that the Lord would make it hard for him, if the Lord was dissatisfied with his association."

The association must have died because I never heard of it again. It turned out that the two ministers at that place were the two which held the meeting previously spoken of.

Once at the South Dakota State Camp Meeting, on account of the weather, we had the services in the chapel. One day a man came who said he was a minister. No one knew him, but he looked like a good man. He asked for the privilege of preaching and it was granted him. After he had been preaching a while it was evident to all that he was badly confused, so the spiritual ones commenced to lift their hearts in prayer to God to stop him, which He did, insomuch that he left the platform and went to the stove to spit, trying to clear his throat. However, there was nothing in his throat. He tried again to speak, but he could not, so finally went out and left the grounds. We never saw him again.

Brother Thomas Nelson and I held a meeting in Wisconsin and we had the same kind of an experience as the one given above. The man in this case was a professor in college and a real orator, but his religious doctrine was unscriptural. Brother Nelson and I had given him the privilege of preaching. We gave one another an understanding glance to be agreed in prayer asking God to stop him immediately. He lost his voice and could not continue speaking.

———— : : : : ————

DISCOURAGEMENT BLINDS A PERSON

At one time I was holding a meeting at Badger, South Dakota. The meeting was fairly good in a way but I expected results and hoped to see souls saved. I worked and fasted and prayed, but to no avail. It seemed there was no conviction upon sinners. When that meeting was over, I decided to quit the ministry, thinking to myself, "What is the use to go on this way, enduring hardships and sufferings and not seeing any souls saved." I thought I must be a failure, so going home, I went through Minneapolis, Minnesota to visit my sister. After the evening meal I thought I would take a walk. As I strolled up Lake Street, I saw to my left in the middle of the block, a large sign, 'Revival Meetings, Minnesota's Greatest Evangelist.' I became interested because I had lived in Minnesota many years and had never heard his name before, so I decided to attend. By the time he was half through his sermon, my discouragement had vanished. I thought, "I'm a better preacher than that; I can preach the Truth." So I went back to preaching with fresh courage and determination.

The next year just before the Minnesota State Camp Meeting at St. Paul Park, I came home with another load of discouragement. It seemed to me I was backslidden and that Brother Nelson and Brother Tubbs were going to deal with me at the meeting and tell me so. I told wife to go on to the meeting and I would stay home and rest a few days, as I was tired. She objected and refused to go without me, telling me the saints would be asking about me, and if I told them you were home they would be wondering why and I would have no peace, so that was that. We went and I did not attempt to preach neither Saturday, Sunday, nor Monday. I was waiting, expecting the brethren to come and have a talk with me. Finally on Monday afternoon Bro. Nelson came and said, "Let us go out into the timber. I want to have a talk with you." Then he said, "Brother Susag, what is the matter with you? You are holding up the meeting. Everyone is expecting you to preach and you sit there and say nothing." I answered, "Yes, I know that you know what it is." "Why I don't know anything," he said, "What do you mean?" I said, "Aren't you and Bro. Tubbs going to deal with me? You know I am backslidden." "Since when?" he asked. I told him I did not know. He then said, "We surely do not know anything. It is just an imposition of the devil. Rebuke him and get into the pulpit and preach." We had prayer, and rebuked the devil and his accusations, and the spell was completely broken.

A year later at the Minnesota State Camp Meeting, Brother Nelson was not feeling well, neither was I. One day, Brother Nelson said to me, "What do you think is the trouble with us? Maybe we are bad boys." I told him, "No, that is not the reason, however, we do not see many healings and miracles now." As we stood there talking, we could not think of anything that had taken place of late.

Just then a sister came up to where we were and said, "Praise the Lord, brethren." We said, "Amen." "I do not suppose you know me?" "Yes, we know you," we said, "But we have forgotten your name." "My name is Rasmussen," she said; "I haven't seen you, Brother Nelson, since you were down and prayed for our youngest son who was down with double pneumonia." Brother Nelson said, "The Lord healed the boy, didn't He?" "I should say He did," she answered. "He not only healed him, but changed him from a puny, delicate child to a strong, husky child—the healhiest one we have." She went away and we felt we had gotten a reproof, and yet an encouragement, from the Lord.

Then a brother came along and he said, "Praise the Lord. Wasn't it wonderful how the Lord restored Brother Krutz?" That was another reproof. Then a sister came by and said, "Have you heard about Sister Johnson?" We asked, which Johnson, and she said, "Brother Morris Johnson's mother. She fell and broke her leg just above the ankle and they took her on the train to St. Paul and while waiting in the Union Depot for a train for home, saints came on their way to the camp meeting and seeing her suffering they had compassion on her, and prayed the prayer of faith, and she was instantly healed, insomuch that she went back to the camp meeting." After she left, Brother Nelson started one direction for the timber and I the other. We felt the Lord had been grieved because of our discouragement and had reproved us in this way.

———— : : : : ————

On Sunday morning while I was holding a meeting at Rice Lake, I was preaching on the Joy of the Lord. After speaking a few minutes, the Lord spoke to me and said, "Your theme today will be trials and discouragements," so I announced to the congregation that the Lord had changed my subject, and in my talk, I related some of the worse trials and discouragements I had passed through. After I was through speaking, a brother came up to the pulpit and said, "Shame on you, Brother Susag." I said, "Say that again." He did a little stronger than before, so I said, "Say it again, for 'all good things are three.' " Then he did say it strong. He said, "Here you have been standing here telling that preachers get tried and tempted and discouraged like that—" and he turned and went out. When he had gone, a young lady came up and asked me for dinner and said, "Brother and Sister — were coming to dinner, too." On arriving at their home, they all sat down to visit. They didn't take off their wraps, nor ask me to either. They said to me, "Do you know why the Lord changed your subject today?" I told them it must have been for somebody. "Yes," they said, "It was for the four of us." (These four had gotten saved in the revival I had held the year before). "We have been tempted and tried so much," they said, "so we came near giving up." Then they said to one another, "Look at Brother Susag. He is happy all the time. He is not tried and tempted like we are." But when they heard of my experiences, they said, "The shame is on us." They were much encouraged and went on in the service of God. They finally moved somewhere to the northwest and I am told that one of the brothers became a minister and the other three Sunday School workers.

 Many people do not realize that ministers pass through much suffering both spiritual and physical for the sake of others, but they are glad to do so for Christ's sake and for the sake of others.

 While pastoring in Grand Forks, North Dakota a lady called on the phone one day and asked to speak to The Rev.

Susag. "I am the one speaking," I said. Then she told me she had heard from Mrs. Werstlein that I would pray for anyone no matter what church they belonged to. I told her I would. Then she said, "My husband is at the Catholic hospital and the doctor just called up and said he is liable to die any minute, and cannot live longer than until three o'clock this afternoon. He is an infidel." Then she continued, "Would you kindly go see him and talk to him and then come by the house as I'd like to hear what he had to say and what you think about it." I told her I would if I could get in to see him. "Tell them that I sent you," she said. At first they refused to let me in, but after telling them I was pastor and that his wife had sent me they said alright. They said, "He is near death and almost has one foot in the grave."

When I went into his room and saw how bad he was, I introduced myself to him and said, "I'm sorry to find you in such a condition. I have been where you are now. I will not tire you out with much talk, but would you let me read you a scripture lesson and pray with you?" He answered, "It would be out of place to refuse such an offer under such circumstances." So I read Jesus' conversation with Nicodemus. (John 3:1) Then I knelt and prayed a short prayer. When I got through, he put his hand out and said, "Thank you, I have got to see you in the morning." I asked him what time and he told me nine o'clock. Then I bid him good-bye and went to the door. When I reached the door I thought I heard him say something and turned and said, "Beg your pardon, did you say something?"

He said, "Can I depend on you?" I answered, "Yes, you can depend on me, and furthermore we have service tonight in the church, and I will tell the folks to agree in prayer for you and also to fast and pray tomorrow that the Lord will heal you." He thanked me and I left him.

When I went to his house, his wife said, "What do you think about my husband?" I answered, "He is pretty low, but I am going back to see him tomorrow morning at nine o'clock." She said, "He isn't going to live that long." I told her he was not going to die, but going to live, and she said, "Who said so?" I answered, "The Lord."

Next morning I went back and eight nurses met me and one said, "What did you do to that man yesterday? He had one foot in the grave and now he is going to live." "Of course he is going to live," I said. Then they said, "But what did you do? We have never seen anything like this." "Well," I said, "I did what they used to do in olden times." "What was that?" they asked. "Prayed," I said. "Yes," they said, "that helps."

Going into his room, he was smiling and I began to talk to him about the Lord. Then he said, "I do not believe in those old women's fables." I said, "I am going to get you to believe in God." He replied, "You can't do it." I answered, "By God's help I can, for where you are, I have been, and where I am, you can come. If I can only gain one point with you I can get you to believe in God." (He was a professor at the University of North Dakota). I had to come back in the afternoon at three o'clock and the next morning at about nine. When I came in he said, "You are too late. The doctor was here with two specialists and I told them I wanted to get up and go home; I am well. They answered me, 'You stay in bed; you are a sick man. There are no T B germs about you but we are studying about what kind of medicine to give you.' " He then asked me how I would have answered them, if I had been here, and I said to him, "I would have said to them, 'The God of

Heaven that you don't believe in, heard prayers and smote those germs and made you well.'" He said, "If you had told them that, there would have been a panic."

The next morning he got up and went home. I was sent to Europe on a special mission the next day by the Missionary Board and the church. After returning in January, one Monday morning I went to the Northern State Bank on business and on opening the door into the bank, who should I meet, but this professor. My hands went up and I said, "Glory to God! Here is the man the Lord kept out of the grave last August." Up went his hands, and he said, "Bless God. God Almighty did something for me."

———— : : : : ————

I regret that I have not kept a record through the years. The only record I have is for the first eleven months. I was pastor in Brookings and White, South Dakota. I preached 272 sermons, made 178 pastoral visits, wrote 202 letters, traveled almost fifteen thousand miles during that time, and in my fifty years ministry, have had a stated salary only about six years. In my first ten to fifteen years, I preached (at intervals) as many as six sermons a day, three in Norwegian and three in English. In all I have preached something over 17,000 sermons, and have traveled over one million miles. I have crossed the Atlantic Ocean seventeen times one way, and preached a good many times on fifteen of those voyages.

———— : : : : ————

Returning to America in the late fall of 1939, many people asked me who I thought was to blame for the war. They named a number of the leading rulers of the warring nations, and then they added, "The devil." I said, "None of them are to blame for the war." "Who then?" they asked. "Backslidden, professing Christians," I said. Then they asked if I thought America would get into it, and I answered, "Most assuredly." However the majority of them said no, and they also said that our American boys would never leave American soil to fight. I told them that our boys would not only go to Europe to fight, but to almost all the Islands of the sea. Then they asked how long I thought the war was going to last, and I told them "1949." A goodly number laughed me to scorn. Not long ago, I received a letter from my oldest son who said, "I have been checking up on you dad and everything that you said would happen, has come true up to the present date." The actual fighting is over, but thousands of our men are in foreign lands, and no peace. If the Lord does not get an opportunity to perform a miracle, another war will start before any real peace.

I have not built any chapels large or small, but I have started about fifty or more congregations in this country (America) and in Europe. Also I have raised quite a sum of money to build chapels and to help ministers and missionaries in need. I have raised thousands for church and missionary work in general, seventy per cent has come from the brethren of Norwegian descent, fifteen percent from the Danish descent, ten percent from those of German descent, three percent from the Swedish, and two percent from Americans. The percent here mentioned is for the work in Scandinavian countries only.

———— : : : : ————

While holding a meeting in Bowbells, North Dakota, after a few days three families quit coming and I went out to the farm to see them. When I arrived at the first farm, the other two families were there visiting. After conversing a while, I asked them why they had not been out to the services of late. Finally the man who was the head of the house said, "We did not like it when you said the preacher could not forgive sins." I answered, "If you have wronged the preacher, and ask him his forgiveness he can forgive you, but there are some sins that even the Lord cannot forgive. For instance, if you owe ten dollars to your neighbor over the hill, and you are not willing to pay him, you can keep on praying as long as you live, and the Lord could not forgive you if you are not willing to settle with him. Of course, if you didn't know where he was and couldn't find him, the Lord would forgive you all right." The man answered, "We will come to the services," they said, and some of them got saved. Unbeknown to me, he had owed his neighbor ten dollars for four years and was unwilling to pay, but after he became willing he got saved and paid his debt.

———: : : :———

One man got saved in a meeting in South Dakota, and the Lord reminded him of twelve ears of corn which he had taken from his neighbor's field to feed his own oxen. As he went by on his way to town, he said, "Yes, I'll attend to that tonight." So after dark he filled a bushel basket with corn and took it over and emptied it into the man's hog pen, feeling good that he had done his duty. The next morning after worship, the Lord spoke to him and said, "I suppose today you will go over and settle for the twelve ears of corn." "Why I took that over last night," he protested, "But you took that over to the hogs, and they were already fed." So he went over and confessed to the man. We can see by this that it was not the corn the Lord was so interested in as his humble confession.

GOD WORKS IN VARIOUS WAYS FOR THE PROTECTION AND DELIVERANCE OF HIS CHILDREN

A certain brother who was a farmer needed a threshing machine badly, and an agent visited him to see if he could make the deal. They were agreed on prices and terms, but when they talked over the time of delivery, the agent acknowledged he could not get it to him in time for fall threshing, so the deal fell through. Another agent, hearing of it decided he would go and see the farmer. This time the deal went through, with the promise that the machinery would be delivered in time.

The brother mortgaged his farm and the threshing machine for forty five hundred dollars, but when harvest time came it had not come. He wrote the manufacturers, and they said that as soon as they could get it built and shipped, they would do so. The farmer became desperate. He took the sales contract to an attorney, but he found a clause in it that prevented him from doing anything about it. It looked as if he would lose all his threshing income that fall as well as the machine and his farm too. Many earnest prayers went up that the Lord would intervene in his behalf.

During harvest time that year, he lost hundreds of dollars in not having the machine.

Finally in January, the machine was shipped from the factory. The freight train that was pulling it got within three miles of the town. It was pulling up grade slowly, and in turning a sharp curve the whole car which was carrying the threshing machine loosened from the rest of the train, and tumbled down a steep embankment, completely demolishing the whole thing. The railroad paid the damages, and the brother was released from all responsibility.

A good many went out to see the wreckage, and none could understand how the car would become disconnected from the train. They did not know our God, and the way he answers prayer.

———— : : : : ————

When I was holding a meeting at Grand Forks, wife wrote me that an epidemic of small pox had broken out in the neighborhood, but that it was not necessary for me to come home because, she said, "I put the children and myself into the 91st Psalm and we will remain there until the scourge is over" and I thank God, it did not come near our dwelling.

———— : : : : ————

No apology is made for writing this book, recording the incidents and experiences herein found. As Elijah's God is still the God of the universe and today He hears the prayers of the humble and delivers them in time of need. The author is acquainted with the persons mentioned herein, and has a personal knowledge of the things related. No doubt some will question the truthfulness of some of the statements made in this volume. But the truth must not be withheld because of a few skeptics and unbelievers. Some doubted the miracles wrought by the apostles. One good minister in California said one time, when introducing me to the ministers at a ministers' meeting, "This brother can relate more incidents than anyone I have ever known, and if I did not know Brother Susag, as well as I do, I would have said he lied." I answered, "If I did not know him as well as I do, I would have said he lied, too."

Brother C. E. Brown, present editor of the Gospel Trumpet, upon introducing me to a number of ministers at the Anderson Camp meeting, also stated that I could relate more actual incidents and experiences than anyone he had ever met.

Many ministers and the laity as well, have through the years wanted me to write a book of my experiences, even ministers of other movements. But I am afraid I have waited too long to remember hundreds of incidents that have taken place during my ministry. People say that when I am under the anointing of the Holy Ghost when preaching, the incidents flow from my lips like a stream.

My earnest humble prayer is that these incidents and experiences may prove a blessing and an inspiration that will quicken the faith of those in need whose help can come only from God.

As my name is S. O. Susag, I think it is fitting to say as the distress call of a ship is SOS, that I have heard the distress call in my fifty-two years ministry, hundreds of times from the evangelistic field, and missionary fields in other lands, from insane asylums, hospitals, sick rooms, and the Lord has heard prayer, and wrought many miracles, almost unbelievable. To God belongs all the glory and praise.

——— : : : : ———

One time I received a distress call from Geo. W. Green and family who were living that time on a farm near Hancock, Minn., to come and pray for a sick child. They were living six or seven miles out of town, and no one was there to meet me, so I had to get the taxi to take me out. I arrived late in the evening. Going into the house, I learned the child was already dead. All the occupants of the house, both up and down stairs, were sick in bed with the flu, thirteen in all. Sister Green was the only one able to get out of bed to let me in. I had no way to get back to town, but as we were talking and praying, a doctor happened along and stopped and came in and asked Sister Green to make him a strong cup of coffee and sandwich. He said, "This is the third night since I was in bed, and I need something to strengthen me." He filled out a burial permit for the child so it could be buried. And he said, "You can't stay here tonight." I told him I had no way to get back to town, so he offered to take me. I went and the next day I returned with the undertaker. The road to the cemetery went through the town, but the leading lady, a social worker (I presume) forbad us taking the body through town. So we had to detour several miles out of our way. An epidemic of flu broke out in the town and I am told that this lady was the first one to die with it. At the Green home the Lord restored the entire thirteen to health, and protected me. Throughout the years I have been protected from all manner of contagious diseases where I have been called to pray.

———— : : : : ————

Brother Edward Ahrendt and I were holding a meeting in Grand Forks, North Dakota. One evening the call was made, and the altar was filled with seekers. Brother Ahrendt and I started at opposite ends to pray and instruct. As I knelt, the first one was a woman and I felt as if I had knelt by a barrel of devils. I was surprised that she was professing to be a Christian. Lifting my hand in astonishment, I said, "Sister G—you are possessed with devils." After the altar service was over, Brother Ahrendt and I laid our hands on her and commanded the devils to come out in the name of

Jesus, which they did. The next morning we had prayer and testimony meeting and she arose and testified and in a way she excused herself. I said, "Sister, be careful or the devils will enter into you again." Evidently they did, because the other women in the rooming house told me that in the evening when she arrived at her room to go to bed, the devils rolled her up like a ball with her heels almost on her shoulders, and her sufferings were horrible. They prayed and did everything they could to help her get straightened out, but to no avail. They tried to find Bro. Ahrendt and I, but we had moved that night to another place. No one seemed to know where we were. They called up all the saints that had phones, but without success. Finally, two of the sisters started out going from house to house among the saints that had no phones, and at four o'clock in the morning they reached the house where we were stopping. We went over as quickly as possible, and when we went up onto the porch, she straightened out instantly. The devil was going to play possum on us. Brother Ahrendt and I had a consultation, as he had never had any experiences with cases of devil possession before. He said, "Brother Susag, Saturday night when we prayed for her, there was no manifestation showing that she was possessed." "Well," I said, "There is no need of them having to be thrown around by the devil when you know they are possessed," so I said I would pray and we would see how it would come out, because I knew there was a need of full agreement. We phoned Brother Gus Niles and asked if we could come to his place with Mrs. G—. When we got there, we went into a room and locked the doors. Brother Ahrendt prayed in one corner and Brother Niles in another corner. I gave her a chair by the table, and I sat opposite. I said, "Sister, I have known you for four years and all that time you have deceived yourself and the saints and the ministry. You have had no salvation all this time. Now tell me what the devil had you do when you came home from meetings." She said, "One time when I came home, I went out to the barn to feed milk to the calf, and he wouldn't drink, and I got angry and took a small club and struck him. He bawled and broke the rope and jumped through the window and ran out into the woods." When she was telling this, her hand flew up and she commenced beating the air with it and she could not stop. I let her continue beating for a time, then I said, "Lord, stop that arm," and it did stop. Then I asked her what the devil got her to do other times when she came home. She said, "Another time when I came home, husband's dog had gotten into the house, and I opened the door to get him out, and as he went through the door, I kicked him in anger because I hated my husband," and as she said this, she started kicking the table and then she fell on the floor on her back still kicking the chair and the table. Just then Brother Ahrendt came running and said, "I rebuke the devil in Jesus' name." He had become convinced that the devils were there by now.

Then the three of us laid hands on her, commanding the devils to come out of her, which they did. Then she got saved and sanctified, and got a sweet settled experience which everyone had confidence in. She later became an able Sunday School teacher and worker for the Lord.

———— : : : : ————

A WARNING

The evening when I said, "Sister G, you are possessed with devils," I looked back in the audience and saw a sister with her mouth open and looking at me with surprise and apparent criticism, as if to say, "What do you mean by saying such things to Sister G?" Just then I saw many serpents crawling in her lap and up her breast and in to her mouth. After the service this woman's sister came to me and said, "Do you know that my sister, Mary, is possessed with devils?" I said, "Yes," and she asked how I knew, saying, "She told me she had just gotten possessed. I said, "I saw them entering."

We took her to a private home and she was delivered by the power of God.

———: : : :———

There is always a cause when God does not answer prayer, either in individuals or congregations. I have been speaking of individual cases in this book, where prayer was not answered. Now I will speak of congregational hindrances that I know of personally.

There is never an effect without a cause that produces the effect. In a certain congregation where I held several successful revivals for several pastors, there came a time when the work did not prosper as it had in previous years. By chance after twenty years absence, I stopped in there one prayer meeting night, having business in the town that day. They entreated me to come back and speak for them on a certain Sunday, which I did. The Lord gave us two precious services. They took up their regular Sunday evening offering. After that, they announced that they would take up an offering especially for Brother Susag, which they did, and set the basket in a position where I noticed the contents, which was in the neighborhood of fifteen dollars or a little more. Next morning when I was ready to take the train, I was handed four dollars with the remark, "This is our custom." No wonder the congregation did not prosper, and still these dear people had done their duty, but were unaware of what the hindrance was.

I know of other cases of that same kind, both with other ministers and myself. Once in a camp meeting a young minister was the evangelist, whom the Lord used mightily. One evening they were going to take up the love offering for the evangelist. A nice offering came in, not any too large, and they gave the evangelist seventy percent.

———: : : : ———

Once at the Grand Forks, North Dakota Camp Meeting, Brother P. Pederson of Hoboken, New Jersey was to preach. He read his text and related some of his experiences and the Holy Ghost began to bring the people to the altar. He then closed his Bible and said, "A greater preacher than I is now speaking."

———: : : : ———

During the depression it looked as though we were going to lose the state camp grounds at Grand Forks. At the camp meeting the Board said there is no other way than to let it go. I said, "No." "Well," they said, "Then you will have to raise the money because we cannot." I said, "If you will give me a free hand, to go at it when the Lord says to, I will." They said O. K. One evening the Lord said, "Now is the time," so I said to Brother Monk, "Let me have a few minutes?" Within a few minutes we had the amount to the cent. Brother Monk said, "This time the devil was licked and the depression also." It pays to pray.

———: : : : ———

The first Camp Meeting I attended at Grand Forks, I generally got up at 3 or 4 a.m. and went to the woods to pray. At that time you could hardly find a place to pray.

There were two or three members praying behind every tree before I got there.

The first Camp Meeting I attended in Anderson, I went out early in the cemetery and here they were praying every where.

The pioneer ministers knew how to pray, because they had no sermon outline book to take it from. Their converts knew how, too, for they were taught by the Holy Ghost.

———: : : :———

Once Brother Renbeck and I were holding a meeting in Erskine, Minn. It was 42 degrees below zero every day, and we had to stand the bread by the heating stove and a number of times it froze so hard on the table, before we got through with our meal, that we could not eat it. When we went to bed, we could see the stars twinkling through the cracks of the roof. We took off our shoes and coats and lay down on the bed, and pulled our fur caps down over our ears and put our fur coats over us. Often through the night we would have to turn over because the side that was down got cold. This may seem ridiculous to some, but God knows it is true.

———: : : :———

In 1911 Brother Morris Johnson and I held a meeting on the west coast of Denmark. At the place where we stayed and slept, we had to climb up a ladder through a hole into the room to sleep. The bed was too short for Bro. Johnson and too narrow for two, and the bed clothes accordingly.

We could not sleep much after breakfast. We took our traveling blankets and walked out side the town where there were some old grave hills that had been opened to get out the wealth that was buried. It left a deep hollow place in the ground. There was ice in the bottom. We wrapped our blankets around us and lay down so the wind could not blow on us and slept some. That was pioneering in Denmark. In this little town it was really the first great battle for the truth won in Denmark.

Many have said that much of the pioneer work was lost and did not pay. It is true, some was lost, but what would we have had today without it? I pray God to rekindle the pioneer spirit and passion for souls and trust in the Lord. The opportunities are still here. If I were a young man I would say with the prophet, "Here am I, send me."